THERE

&

BACK

by
Terry Michaels

A true story of innocence lost
... and innocence found.

Dedication

To my Lord, Jesus Christ...
for getting me there and back.

CONTENTS

A Thought Before

KEEP CHURCH WEIRD

Austin, Texas is the only city I know of that takes being weird seriously. I am not sure if 'Keep Austin Weird' is the city's official motto but it is a popular one. Apparently, Austinites have embraced their many quirks, so much so they are on a mission to make 'weird' fashionable. It would even appear that if you don't have something weird to contribute to Austin you just don't belong. Only in this strange city could a cigar smoking, Jewish cowboy named *Kinky* have a shot at the governor's seat.[1] Other strange people from Austin have also sought political office, like Leslie, who takes weird to a level perhaps too extreme for your average weirdo.

I had heard about Leslie but never laid eyes on him until recently. He was strolling down Austin's infamous 6th Street. I recognized him right off. From the neck up Leslie looks like your typical vagabond. His hair is long, wiry and disheveled. A mass of scraggly whiskers climb wildly out of his leathery face like tentacles. Admittedly, this does not sound terribly peculiar but believe me, it gets even weirder. Leslie has breasts. I don't know if his endowments are the product of genetics, surgery or clever padding. I do know that he fills out the top of his T-shirt like a calendar girl. Please understand, I am not judging Leslie, I'm merely making a feeble attempt to describe what I saw. It is true, I saw a bearded man with breasts strolling down 6th Street wearing nothing but a T-shirt and thong bikini. My wife is my witness. Oh, how I wish she had not been a witness but she was, and that is the sad truth of the matter. My sources tell me that Leslie took 5% of the vote when he ran for mayor. Only in Austin!
I do not live in Austin. It is not that I am opposed to weird people; I'm just not comfortable with crowds whether they be weird or

---

[1] *Kinky Friedman, 2006 Independent candidate for Governor of Texas*

otherwise. Therefore, I live outside this bustling city, about thirty miles south of weird. I do not deny that I also have some odd quirks but I only contributed to keeping Austin weird for a few brief hours on September 9, 2006. It was the evening when Copeland played at Stubb's. My daughter, Birdie, is a huge Copeland fan so we drove her and a friend up to catch their show. There was a long line of weird people waiting to get into Stubb's when we arrived. They came in all shapes, sizes and colors. According to Birdie these young concert crashers are the 'Emo' crowd. I was grateful that she educated me in this area. My previous understanding was that Emo was a character on *Sesame Street* not a movement on 6th Street. I was tickled to discover that Emo and Elmo are not the same thing.

My wife and I did not join our teenage daughter at Stubbs. I regret to say that Birdie didn't seem too disappointed by this. She has this idea that it would have been too weird even by Austin standards. This is quite perplexing to me; it is acceptable for a man with breasts to strut 6th Street in a thong but parents can't be seen with their own flesh and blood at a Copeland concert. Though I have been accused of being weird myself it seems I have much to learn on the subject.

To kill time Christy and I ventured off to the luxurious Driscoll Hotel for a bite to eat. It is a very nice hotel with a very nice café. The Driscoll is not what you would typically think of as weird. However, as I have already noted I am no expert on the subject. Personally, I do find it odd that someone would pay three to four hundred dollars a night to stay on 6th Street. This tells me that some weird people have money. Lots of it! Then there are the less privileged weird people just a few short blocks away from the Driscoll. They have no money at all and spend nights on wafer thin cots at the homeless shelter. Weird knows no boundaries.

There were other strange happenings on that bizarre September 9, 2006. Ohio State was playing the Texas Longhorns. It appeared as though the whole city of Austin flooded to 6th Street to support their team. As a sign of loyalty, they were all color coordinated in orange. Now, this I found to be especially weird, that an entire population of people would dress alike and show up in the same neighborhood together. Perhaps you have to be a football fan to understand this kind of odd behavior. Many Texans are but I am not. That may have been a result of being raised by my mother with two older sisters, which would also explain why I find malls more exciting than football stadiums and buying new shoes more thrilling than touchdowns. Perhaps I really do belong in Austin!

We saw many weird people there that night: a wannabe minstrel who thought he could sing, a geriatric wizard balancing peculiar things on his nose and a young street urchin with a 'fro the size of Texas. We saw drunks and punks and I think a few monks. Weird grew strangely familiar to us. As I thought about this something began to dawn upon me. The weird thing about Austin is the people who call it home. Other than that it's just a spread of land with ordinary streets and your usual buildings, not much different from any other town. I've never known anyone to look at a map of Austin or pictures of Austin and come to the conclusion it's an odd place. You won't discover that until you start meeting its people.

This has caused me to ponder my own weirdness. I am a pastor but probably not what you would consider your typical pastor. On occasion I meet with other clergy in my community and I readily recognize that I am quite different. It is my impression that they can spot this as well. Most other pastors in my county have conservative haircuts; I shave my head. They dress in slacks; I wear jeans. They like dressy, button-up shirts, I prefer T-shirts. They were formally schooled in theology I am not. Not because I think it is a bad thing it's just that I never intended to go into ministry. God called me later in life. Weird, I know.

Furthermore, it's my conviction that if we are doing church right we won't end up with a house full of people wearing the same colored T-shirts. It seems to me that the more we love like Jesus the more weird our churches will become. If we are truly demonstrating Christ-like compassion our churches will look more like 6th Street than Wall Street. They will be places of refuge where Jewish cowboys, Copeland fans and lonely street minstrels will find acceptance. And dare I say the doors would be open to the Leslie's of the world too, so long as their pants were left on.

It is true, I am no theologian. I never attended seminary nor have I even taken a single class at a Bible college. But I have studied the gospels. I have examined all four intently and carefully, with the scrutiny of a true Berean. My studies have taught me something about Jesus; He surrounded Himself with weird people. All twelve apostles were complete oddballs. Mary Magdalene was like many of the girls you see on 6th Street. As for Zacchaeus, he was completely out of his tree! It wasn't just the ordinary folk who were attracted to Jesus, the weird also adored Him. It would seem that all those who followed Jesus had this one thing in common: they longed for acceptance, something most religious leaders were in short supply of. Acceptance was a rare commodity in New Testament times. But Jesus was different. He accepted anyone willing to come to Him. No one was ever turned down because they were too weird.

As for Austin, it doesn't matter to me whether the city remains weird or not. But speaking as a person with a passion for God this is my heart, 'Keep Church Weird'. I believe this would also be the heart of Jesus who is Lord of the weird and Lord of all. The day we worry about who enters the church doors is the day we need to shut them for good.

Preface

You will quickly note that this book is autobiographical in nature. However it is not a typical biography. Through these pages you will read personal reflections of my wayward youth, some humorous, others dramatic and a few downright tragic. Rather than record detailed narrative that segues from one endless chapter to the next I have chronicled only the highlights, passing over my life rather quickly. This is a photo album of sorts where you turn each page and examine the snapshots. It is not a film which runs continuously from scene to scene. In this photo album you now hold every picture tells my story. It is a story which follows a troubled teen into the arms of his loving Savior.

Chapter 1

FOR A QUARTER I WILL

My older brother Rick and I were raised for the most part in a single parent home. Our folks divorced before the training wheels came off our little red bicycles. Mom never did remarry and was left to manage a household of four unpredictable siblings single-handedly. Dad moved on right away with a young blonde secretary from KTLA, Los Angeles, where he anchored the evening news. Rosey and Dad had already started a family together prior to the divorce, which helps to explain why Mom parted company with him. My sisters Kathy and Karen were practically adults when the split happened so there were no custody battles involving them. As for Rick and I, we were just pups, so our fate rested on the wisdom of a court order. Mom found herself having parental custody eleven months out of the year while Dad enjoyed my brother and me for all of August. This never really sat well with Rosey though. She endured the two of us like a charley horse.

My father's profession as a broadcast journalist took him all over California where he worked major market radio or TV, sometimes even both. Rick and I sang to the tune of the Johnny Cash song, 'I've Been Everywhere' as we followed Dad from L.A. to San Francisco to San Diego and finally the big OC. From the time I was nine years old my big brother and I bounced around the state, spending thirty-plus days of summer with dear old Dad and his contemptuous second wife. But this all came to a screeching halt after the big blow out in 1970, just days before my fourteenth birthday.

Rick and I were never big fans of Rosey. We took to her like cats take to the bathtub. This unscrupulous woman played a key role in breaking Mom's heart and wrecking our happy home. That's just the way we saw it. But it was no secret that Rosey resented us too; she made that quite clear from day one. The first time Rick and I were introduced to Dad's secret family was at the Disneyland Hotel. "Meet your stepmother, Rosey, and your sister, Tabitha," Dad smiled as if there was nothing bizarre about this whole weird scenario. Yet it was very odd having a four-year-old girl being introduced as a sibling. Neither of us asked any questions though, we just rolled with it.

Later that afternoon Rick and Tabitha found themselves kneeling on cheap hotel carpet playing Candyland. She didn't like the fact that he was winning and yelled, "Mom, Rick is cheating!" Without the benefit of hearing from the defense Rosey snapped, "That's because he's nothing but a big cheater!" Needless to say, the accusation really ticked my brother off. "I'm not a cheater," he fired back, "You are!" How could she argue when Rick was glaring across a game board at living evidence? Regardless of this undisputable fact, the comment was not well received; Rosey went on a tirade as she put Rick back in his place. We were not setting a good precedent for our future relationship.

As the evening grew late we were all shown to our beds. Rick and I were given the foldout sofa with inviting metal springs while Dad and the gals sunk into soft and cozy mattresses in a separate room. The sandman had not visited the sofa bed as early as expected so Rick and I engaged in a little whispering. It wasn't long before we heard Rosey yell, *"SHUT UP!"* This came as quite a shock to us. We had been taught never to use such phrases, and they were certainly never part of Mom's vocabulary. I asked Rick, "Do you think she was talking to us?" My brother was certain Rosey must have been joking so we continued our quiet talk. *"SHUT UP!"* Rosey yelled again. "I guess she's serious," Rick frowned. That was the end of our conversation.

This continued to be the dynamic of our relationship with Rosey for years to come. But instead of doing weekends in hotels, we dwelt together in the same house for weeks at a time. Things were always cordial in our dealings with Dad; he was pretty good-natured. I think there may have been a conscious effort on his part to compensate for all the ill treatment we received from Rosey. He rarely raised his voice at us. But somehow Rick and I ended up with the same wicked stepmother who plagued Cinderella. I wish I could say things got better. By the time 1970 rolled around things came to a head and August ended early in the OC.

2

Two weeks into our stay I felt a little homesick and pulled out the trusty pen. I wrote a letter to Mom and a couple of neighbor friends. It happened that Rosey was headed out for the post office that same afternoon. "Would you mail these for me, please?" I asked handing her exactly three envelops. She took the letters, looked at them then handed them back. "Sorry," she sneered. "I'm afraid I can't." This came as quite a shock to me. "Why not?" I inquired with a puzzled look. "They don't have stamps!" she snapped. "Don't they sell stamps at the post office?" I pressed. "Sorry, can't afford it." was her answer. I was amazed; Dad and Rosey could afford a luxurious home in a gated community on Newport Beach, they could afford a yacht and a membership at the Balboa Bay Club but they didn't have enough funds for stamps at eight cents a pop! As you can imagine I was a little irritated; not just with Rosey but with Dad as well. He had overheard the entire conversation and, apparently, didn't feel I was worth the twenty-four cent investment either.

Later when dinnertime rolled around Rosey told Tabitha to set the table. She snapped, "No, I don't want to!" Rosey did not want to get into it with Tabitha so she told me to set the table. "Okay," I agreed, "For a quarter I will!" I'd even do it for twenty-four cents if she said *pretty please* but I wasn't going any lower. "If you don't set the table you don't get dinner!" Rosey barked. I stood my ground insisting, "If I don't get a quarter I don't set the table!" Things went downhill from there. My dad got involved by taking Rosey's side and chastising me. I must admit, this threw me for a loop. All I wanted to do was mail out three lousy letters and somehow I was the villain. *Had everyone gone postal?* "Look," I finally blurted. "If I can't write my mom or my friends then I want to be with them. I'm packing my bags and leaving." It wasn't a threat. I was going to thumb my way from Newport Beach all the way back to L.A.

While I packed, Rick defended my righteous cause. "Just let him mail the letters," he pleaded. But neither Dad nor Rosey would budge on the matter. Things just escalated and got uglier. "Pack my bags too!" Rick called. As he continued to fight the good fight I loaded our luggage. Before long we were on Pacific Coast Highway with thumbs out and suitcases by our sides. Dad pulled up a little later, opened the

3

passenger door then told us to get in. "Don't talk to strangers," Rick instructed me as he kicked the door shut. My father got the hint and slowly drove off. In less than twenty minutes he returned. This time he rolled down the window. "Come on in, I'll drive you home in the morning," he gasped with a defeated look on his face. After much debate Rick and I finally conceded and got in the car. That night Rosey vowed to us, "This is the last time you'll ever stay here."

Because Mom was on vacation in Mexico with my oldest sister Kathy, Dad couldn't take us home. So Rick and I were dropped off at our sister Karen's house in San Diego. It was there that I celebrated fourteen bumpy years of youth. Dad did not acknowledge my birthday that year nor would he ever remember another birthday of mine. And the words of Rosey rang true. That doleful August of 1970 was the last time Rick and I were ever invited back to the big OC.

Chapter 2

ANGEL ON THE BOULEVARD

I really don't know when I got saved. I was either fourteen or twenty-two, I'm not sure which. I guess it really depends upon your point of view. You see, I accepted Christ at fourteen, walked away from Him at fifteen, then returned to Him seven years later. This book chronicles those seven lost years, there and back, from Jesus to the mire then back to Jesus again. Now, you may think I was saved at fourteen while others would argue that had I died prior to my twenty-second birthday I would have surely roasted in the fiery abyss. Maybe you're wondering which position I take, was I *heaven bound* or *hell bound* as a young fella'? I'd have to answer 'yes' as I'm pretty sure it was one of those. We're you expecting something a little more decisive? Perhaps you were hoping I was the chosen one, the supposed sage who would finally settle this centuries old debate of 'once saved always saved'. That's another book for another time and I'll be sure to submit my manuscript when I'm ready to disclose all the answers to this great mystery. But for now, I will simply tell my story. I will spare you of all my boring theological dissertations concerning eternal security and the sovereignty of God. Rather than preach I prefer to bear testimony to the wonderful grace of God. To do so I must take you there and back, from salvation to rebellion to all out surrender.

Shortly after I celebrated my fourteenth birthday I prayed to receive Jesus. The memory is as vivid as red lipstick on a cleric's collar. It was a warm September night on Van Nuys Boulevard, a popular strip where young people from all over the valley hung out. We called it 'cruising'. It was not only trendy back then it was legal. Eventually cruising was banned because of difficulties with policing those who didn't respect the tradition. The

Boulevard stretched seven miles from one end of the valley to the other. All four lanes filled up with cruisers who spent the evening driving back and forth from Sherman Oaks to Pacoima like they were part of some sort of Mardi Gras for car freaks. If you ever saw the movie *American Graffiti* you have an idea of what I'm talking about. I could relate to this film because I lived it on a regular basis, only I never saw Suzanne Somers waving at me from a T-Bird.

Wednesday night was considered to be club night on the boulevard. Every group claimed their own turf. The surfers parked their Woodys at Jack in the Box, the Low Riders packed the Pep Boys parking lot, preppie's crowded around Bob's Big Boy and the Hell's Angels lined up their choppers at June Ellen's Donut Shop where the Boulevard ended at Ventura in Sherman Oaks. Traffic was always bumper to bumper with all kinds of cherried out cars, vans and trucks, some raised high, others lowered to the ground. Then there were the kids who were too young to drive. They'd cruise the crowded sidewalks on foot. That's what my buddies and I were doing when we were accosted by an Angel. It's true, I'm not kidding.

This fellow by the name of Stan Angel came out of nowhere and started sharing Christ with us. It was the first time I had ever heard a gospel presentation. I believed every word Stan said, I truly did. He totally convinced me I was a sinner and he didn't even need a little stick drawing of a chair inside a circle to do it. I can't speak for my buddies but when Stan led us in the sinner's prayer I truly meant it. Do you remember the story of when Jesus told that Rich Young Ruler to get rid of all his earthly possessions and follow Him? I was right there, believe me. I didn't have any material belongings of worth but I'm sure I would have left them all if I did. I would have followed Jesus I just know it. I also know I would have lasted only a few short

6

blocks before turning back with my tail between my legs. Not that I wasn't sincere when I took up after Jesus, I just had no idea the road was going to be so rough.

The beginning of my journey went pretty smooth. Stan introduced us to a Christian coffee house on the boulevard. I never realized such a place existed but it was always packed, unlike the topless joint next door. From time to time the pitiful patrons from the peep show would venture over in an attempt to die to the flesh and a few of them even got saved. The Mustard Seed became home to a lot of freaky folks. It was a place where misfits like me found acceptance. The people were genuine, they all loved Jesus and I was one of them. I didn't find out until many years later that I had been part of a movement - the Jesus Movement. It's true! A picture in a Jesus People news rag shows me in a crowd of fanatics marching a seventeen-mile stretch from Van Nuys Boulevard all the way to the Sunset Strip in Hollywood. Arthur Blessit led the pack, carrying a huge wooden cross every step of the way. I even held a sign! It said 'One Way!' in big, bold letters. I also passed out little red stickers with happy faces that said, 'Smile God Loves You!' These are things you don't do unless you are radically saved, right?

But in spite of my acts of commitment I didn't stick with it. My faith faded out with the Jesus Movement. Not because the movement ceased to be cool, I just hit too many bumps and finally got sick of it. Some might point to this as evidence I was never saved at all. They would argue that I was the seed which never fell on fertile ground. I would have to say, "True!" The soil wasn't cultivated very well, I admit it. But does this mean I was never saved? I have studied the Parable of the Soils and here is what I see: The seed which never hit the dirt and landed on the wayside was quickly swept up by the enemy. This is the person who rejects the gospel, he was never saved nor was he ever interested in salvation. I didn't fall into that category

7

though. There was also the seed which fell on fertile soil (I'm jumping ahead here, I know.) and this is the guy who receives the Word gladly and bears much fruit. Definitely saved! But there are those other two categories in between: seeds which fall upon rocky soil and get fried out (me), then there are seeds which fall in thistles and get choked out. But it is never suggested that they aren't saved or lose their salvation. Jesus simply states that the one who fries out *falls away* and the one who gets choked out *is unfruitful.*

Though Jesus never stated that the 'fried' or 'choked' were never saved, He never ruled it out either. Let's face it; there are those that get on the Christian bandwagon who are insincere from the get-go. And for some, their decision is nothing more than an emotional response to an altar call given by some charismatic super stud with an Elvis jacket. Maybe some were drunk as a skunk at the time. But the fact of the matter is, not everyone who falls from the faith fits into the 'never saved' category. There are sincere people who become believers only to fall away or get choked out by the world. But we don't have the wisdom to decide who's who or which is which; we're simply called to accept people where they are. I've learned these valuable lessons from Jesus' parable: First, salvation is God's work, which He accomplishes through the hearing of His Word. Secondly, some believers are more fruitful than others. Finally, God hasn't put us on fruit patrol or called us to determine who is truly saved and who is not. We're to cast seeds, not stones.

I believe these lessons are both biblical and practical. I further believe that each of us should judge the sincerity of our own heart and the genuineness of our own faith. Personally, I needed to explore why I became fruitless and why I fried out and fell away. I needed to look at the man in the mirror, not to tear down or criticize myself, but as a necessary precaution to insure against falling again. I can summarize why I fell in one sentence: I didn't press into Jesus. I pressed into many good things, mind you. There were a lot of well meaning people around telling me to get into church, get into Sunday school and get into Christian service. However, if there was any voice encouraging me to get into *Jesus*, I did not hear it. This presents an even more searching question: What exactly did I fall away from? Was it from religion or a relationship? If I have learned anything from Jesus' discourse of the *vine and the branches* it is this: our lives can only be fruitful when we are abiding in Christ (Read John 15). Fruitfulness is not a product of religious deeds. The bottom line is this: if you are not abiding in Jesus you will fall. One of the enemy's greatest lies is that we can avoid such tragedies by clinging to the church or other religious stuff. It seems the right way to go but unless we are clinging to Jesus daily, a fall is inevitable. Our Lord taught "Without me you can do nothing." (See John 15:5) The only way to remain standing is to cultivate a relationship with Jesus Christ each day. I did not. I failed to spend any time with Him whatsoever. I was busy doing a lot of stuff like marching and attending services but private worship was not a part of my early Christian experience. So, I fell.

Although I drifted pretty far from God in those lost days I see now that His hand was always on me. He refused to let me get away from Him completely. Before checking out on the Lord I spent about a year of getting acquainted with Him. There was a root or two dangling in fertile soil when I fell into the mire, just enough for God to pull me back. And pull He did, for seven excruciating years.

9

Chapter 3

SOFT RED CUSHIONS

When I was small Mom and Dad dragged me to Catholic Mass each Sunday. When I say dragged, I mean that quite literally. There was nothing about the experience I enjoyed. Nothing! I was required to wear a stiff, starchy suit which I utterly detested. The black strap-on bow tie strangled me to near death and has scarred me for life. To this day I have an absolute aversion to wearing anything around my neck. And what fairy came up with the idea that guys appear more proper with long, silky ribbons around their collars? I wish he'd been strangled! After getting all suited up the six of us would pack ourselves into a Chevy Monza and head for St. Ceril's Church in Encino. Inside it always seemed cold, dark and eerie to me. There I would sit, constrained in my unyielding suit, trying to conform my sore butt to some a hard wooden pew that was older than the combined age of the parishioners. For a full hour my head would spin and swirl into a state of oblivion from the seemingly endless rounds of meaningless chanting.

Through the Mustard Seed I was introduced to a new kind of church, the First Baptist Church of Van Nuys. This experience was extremely surreal for someone who grew up Catholic. For one thing the place was massive unlike the parish I attended as a tyke. I don't know how many hundreds of members the Baptist church sat. Rows upon rows of perfectly lined pews faced a lofty stage where a hefty wooden pulpit proudly stood front and center. Massive organ pipes cascaded down the tall ceiling like twin waterfalls pouring down streams of gold on either side of the baptismal. Furthermore, First Baptist was lively! I say this because I remember St. Cyril's as being very subdued. There was a sacred silence once you crossed the holy threshold. A small, marble basin welcomed the quiet splashes of a thousand eager fingers five at a time. But the Baptist church was quite different. People lingered in the lobby, chatting up a storm and, God forbid, laughing aloud for all to hear! This would have been considered irreverent at St. Cyril's but that was clearly not the case at First Baptist. This was all very curious for a sheltered kid like me. I also remember the sanctuary of the Baptist church being lit up like a grocery store, which gave it a most cheery feel. It conveyed the idea that if God were in the house no one wanted him lurking in the shadows somewhere. And one final thing, the pews were notably different than the ancient ones my young fanny grew to despise. At First Baptist they had soft red cushions you could sink into. These Protestants were truly on to something; a positive church experience begins at the bottom!

I was baptized as a young teen at The First Baptist Church of Van Nuys. It wasn't my idea but it didn't sound like a bad one so I went for it. I still remember that cold night. Afterwards I cussed up a storm in a sea of cars out in the parking lot because I couldn't find my mom and I was impatient to go home. I guess not all my sins were washed away. Perhaps I should have gargled but honestly I don't think rinsing with holy water would have improved my language. It wasn't until many years later that my mouth got born again. Sins of the tongue are hard to lick.

I met a lot of good people through the Baptist Church and its street ministry, the Mustard Seed, many of whom took time to personally invest in my newfound faith. I'll never forget Reverend Harrah, a soft-spoken old gentleman who always greeted me with a welcoming smile. As a rule I typically felt uncomfortable around authority figures, but not with the Rev. Though his words were few, I felt a kindred spirit in him. Then there was the gregarious Jim Allison who drove me to church every Sunday. It was his idea I get baptized and I'm grateful he took such an interest in a squirrelly punk like me. Ric Wonders was another fellow I looked up to. He was a big jolly surfer dude. I often wondered how a fellow his size could stand up on a thin, fiberglass board without ever sinking. Ric was the one who oversaw the Mustard Seed coffee house. I'm not sure what his title was or if he even had one.

Tom Fifer was another reverend who served on staff at First Baptist. He also made a lot of appearances at the Mustard Seed and occasionally taught Bible studies there. There was a small house across from church where Fifer kept his office, this is where he discipled and counseled young people. The little house became known as FAM, short for *family* and an acronym for 'For All Mankind'. Fifer was the first reverend I had ever heard use the expression 'boob' in a sermon. Normally priests didn't say things like boob in their homilies so I found this sort of amusing. Everyone thought Fifer was real cool because he rode a motorcycle, had long hair and always wore Levi 501 blue jeans. I also sported long hair and wore 501 blues but I wasn't cool like Fifer because he had a motorcycle and he could grow a mustache. I didn't get fuzz on my lip until much later.

I could be spotted at the Mustard Seed almost every other night or at the First Baptist Church on any given Sunday. These places offered me a sense of belonging and all the thoughtful people made me feel genuinely cared for. The great thing was I wasn't expected to wear one of those dreadful suits or a torturous necktie! There were those who did suit up for church, mostly the older folks, but kids my age tended to dress very casually, just like the Reverend Tom Fifer. And, if that didn't beat all, I could actually understand the preacher! Every word! This was not always a pleasant thing, mind you. Sometimes he could get a little gruff. And when it came to tithing he'd really hammer that point home. One time I remember him saying, "It doesn't matter to me if you don't put anything in the plate. You're not robbing from me, you're robbing from *GODDD!*" I wasn't too inspired by this so I kept my buck and a half. But these gut wrenching guilt trips did seem to stack the offering plate in his favor.

I would not be who I am today if it were not for The Mustard Seed and the First Baptist Church of Van Nuys. It is through these ministries I was introduced to the essential doctrines of the faith. They helped me gain a better understanding of Jesus and what He did for me. I also learned the benefits of Christian fellowship and that church didn't have to be painful to be spiritual. While it may have been the First Baptist Church that later exposed me to some blatant Christian snobbery it was also here that I was lavished in Christ-like love by guys like Stan Angel, Jim Allison, Reverend Harrah and Ric Wonders. Sad to say though, when you're backsliding you lose sight of gems like these. You tend to focus on the snobs, which I did. But today I'm most grateful for those precious saints who poured themselves into a troubled, ragamuffin punk like me.

Chapter 4

TORN BETWEEN TWO BROTHERS

While love covers a multitude of sins it does not ease the many hurts of a dysfunctional family, not the brand of love our family shared. I suppose that's what makes dysfunctional families the way they are. They strive to grasp, interpret and extend love but somewhere along the line there is a breakdown. Something happens that retards a family's ability to receive and reciprocate a kindred kind of love one to another. That's when families lose control. You see, love is the only stabilizing force available for a household to hold together. There are no substitutes. But when people have been hurt love only trickles out in small increments, this is to prevent even further hurt. The reality is those we love most are capable of hurting us most. Therefore, the broken heart is a guarded one. However, when there is a tight control on love the expected result can only be chaos.

The love the Bible speaks of is one that is completely selfless and absolutely unconditional. This is how love is defined in 1 Corinthians 13: *"Love is patient. Love is kind. Love isn't jealous. It doesn't sing its own praises. It isn't arrogant. It isn't rude. It doesn't think about itself. It isn't irritable. It doesn't keep track of wrongs. It isn't happy when injustice is done, but it is happy with the truth. Love never stops being patient, never stops believing, never stops hoping, never gives up. Love never comes to an end."* My mother was a saint in that she truly served well in modeling this kind of love but 1 Corinthians 13 would not be an accurate description of our overall home environment. Unfortunately Mom didn't have the support of a husband as his love fell more in the category of selfish and conditional. Because the two (Mom and Dad) were not one with respect to love the rest of us became rather confused on the matter.

I am convinced that God designed the family unit to have two complimentary role models for love. There is the tender nurturing love of Mom who kisses boo-boos, bandages scraped knees and lavishes her children with affection and cookies and stories read from atop cheery bedspreads riddled with Ninja Turtles or Hello Kitty cartoons. Then there is the valiant love of a father. He has enough warrior in him to protect his home at all cost and provide for his family by laying down his life in some office, construction site or oil field. Should he abandon his post, a breakdown occurs leaving the family in a state of dysfunction. The same is true if Mom bails. The sad truth is Mom cannot fill the void left by Dad, nor can Dad fit into Mom's shoes. I could explain this reality by saying men are from Mars and women are from Venus but I think it has more to do with how God designed things and assigned distinct roles to two very different genders. I give my mom full credit for doing the best she could. She loved all four of us with every ounce of love she could muster. But as a single mother who worked full time she was stretched to the limit. Our family was not dysfunctional because of any lack of effort on her part. Dad had left his post.

*   *   *   *   *

If you've done the math in chapter one correctly, you probably figured out that I was the youngest of four kids. Presently you hardly know them. I think you will have more appreciation for my story once you are better acquainted, so allow me to formally introduce you.

Kathy, twelve years my elder, was more like a parent to me. I guess she felt it was her responsibility to pick up the slack left by my Dad's absence. When mom wasn't home Kathy would assume her role as well. When I was little Kathy would remind me to wash up before mealtime and tell me to eat my broccoli. She also became my barber and was responsible for a lot of bad haircuts- the rice bowl style. Kathy was much more gifted at mothering than barbering, that's for sure. Her maternal nature didn't create much conflict when Rick and I were small but it wore on us more and more as we grew into our teenage years. Because I was timid I never challenged Kathy much but she and my older brother Rick would get into some terrible altercations. One time they really got into it at dinner. Rick picked up the entire kitchen table with all our meals on it and threw the whole thing over. I ended up with everybody's supper on my lap. I think we had chicken that night.

Karen and I were eight years apart. She wasn't the responsible type like my other sister. Quite frankly, Karen had a wild side. She'd run with the boys, party and come home drunk in the wee hours of the night. She and Kathy didn't get along at all. They, too, would get into some nasty quarrels with yelling, cursing, clawing and hair pulling. The sad thing was they had to share a room. That worked out about as well as pairing Courtney Love up with Queen Victoria. While Kathy was strict with Rick and me, Karen was the complete opposite. She consistently spoiled us. When I got into trouble I'd run to her and she'd generally cover my tracks. Maybe I felt safer with her because she wasn't so scissor happy like our resident butcher, Kathy. Although she lived her life recklessly I was quite fond of Karen. Her heart may have been hard toward Kathy but it was tender toward Rick and me. Unfortunately for us, Karen got her own place in San Diego when she turned eighteen. I was just ten at the time. When she left I cried.

Then there was my big brother, Rick. Though he was only a year and a half older he towered over me most of our teen years. I was the runt. My relationship with Rick got very tense at times. He had a temper as hot as a potter's kiln. When he got mad I usually got my puny little butt kicked. This happened quite regularly. Rick took pride in telling me, "Mouse, I can kick your _ss with my little finger." Then he'd strike a blow with his pinky with the full force of his fist behind it. I knew better than to hit back, I'd only have nine more eager digits to contend with. If Rick was in a good mood our brawls would end with just one punch. Other times he would wail on me. Being the scrawny kid I was, I'd just curl into a fetal position while he'd whack away as if he were ridding a doormat of asbestos. My mother would beg him to stop as his balled up fist crashed upon my tear stained face and frail body. Sometimes Mom would call the man next door to pull him off. If he wasn't available she'd call the police. But it was Jay who finally put an end to this madness.

*   *   *   *   *

Jay Gowers was another fellow who became a regular fixture at The Mustard Seed and First Bap. It wasn't hard to miss him. He was a giant black fellow that stood about six foot four, and even taller in platform shoes, which he wore quite often. As a matter of fact, Jay owned more shoes than most women I knew. He was another one who took me under his wing. I called him 'Big Brother' because, well, he was so darned big! And, secondly, he acted the way I thought a brother should. It felt good to have someone older to look up to that wasn't bent on kicking the crud out of me. At twenty-three he was young enough to be hip but not so old that he was square. Plus Jay was generous with his money. He bought things for me my mom couldn't afford which earned my respect all the more. Also, I felt safe with Jay. He'd chase Rick down the street if he even looked at me wrong.

18

Big Brother Jay was no stranger to dysfunctional families. The truth is his was more whacked out than mine. He grew up watching his dad kick the tar out of his mom and everyone else in the house including him. Jay had four brothers and two sisters who all suffered from the physical and sexual abuse that went on in the home. I knew two of his younger brothers from school and they were a couple of bad mothers, the kind you stay clear of. Years later I would see Jay's youngest brother, Zelen, on the evening news. He was suspected of murdering several patients at a hospital where he worked by injecting them with lidocaine. I'm not exaggerating when I say this family had issues. We're talkin' *big issues!*

By the time I met Jay his dad had gotten the boot. Jay had lived in foster homes as a ward of the court until his father was out of the picture, then he moved back home to rule the roost. He was the only one who had his own room, basically because he paid the bills for this welfare family. Other kids slept in the family room while Zelen bedded down in the dining area. The Gowers' home was always filled with a lot yelling and commotion and most resented Jay because of the weight he carried. But Mrs. Gowers always stood by him because she was very appreciative of his big, fat wallet.

Before long I was spending more time at the Gower's homestead than my own. Even though there was a lot of screaming and hollering going on there, none of it was directed toward me. Jay's house also offered an escape from my antagonistic brother. It almost seemed as if Rick's first order of business each day was to provoke me. He'd wake up and call me things like 'nigger lover' just to egg me on. Because he was so violent and antagonistic I couldn't wait to bail out the door. There would also be hell to pay from Jay if I wasn't there to

19

jump at his every beck and call. He'd lay a huge guilt trip on me and make me think I wasn't a true friend if I wasn't around 24/7.

Without question, Jay also had his own set of baggage. This was no secret to me. And just like I felt I needed him to protect me I was convinced he needed me to protect him from the demons in his life. Do not think I am kidding when I say demons, I mean this quite literally. Jay was demon possessed; at least he made me believe he was. The Baptist Church also led me to think that demon possession was a common phenomenon among the saints. Based upon everything I was told about it, Jay showed all the symptoms. Strange and freaky voices would shriek out of him, he would go blind and act very inappropriately when the 'pervert' spirits came out.

Jay had also convinced me that I was the only one these demons would submit to. For the most part, the badly behaved demons with freaky voices disappeared after I rebuked them in Jesus name. The spirit 'Blindness' was less cooperative, he wouldn't split even in the name of Jesus Christ. So I would have to guide Jay by the hand if he needed to go anywhere. One time a fellow named Derrick saw me guiding Jay down the street by the hand. We knew Derrick from the Mustard Seed. He pulled over to inquire about this odd sight so I explained to him that Jay was demon possessed and that I couldn't cast out the evil spirit. He immediately took us to the FAM house across from First Bap to see Tom Fifer. Tom called some other guys and they all laid hands on Jay. This ranks as one of the scariest experiences of my life. 'Blindness' didn't come out without a fight; he yelled, screamed and cursed like crazy before checking out. Because of this episode I wasn't so interested in seeing *The Exorcist* when it came to theatres. After all, I was practically rooming with the devil. It was terrifying as hell to hang around Jay but he needed me and I needed him.

*   *   *   *   *

Today I reject the idea that Christians can become demon possessed. As believers we have the Spirit of the Almighty God dwelling within us and I don't think He's interested in a roommate. Scripture tells us that we have been 'sealed' with the Holy Spirit. (See Ephesians 1:13) Another expression for that term 'sealed' would be: *secured.* We aren't very secure if evil spirits can overtake us. Personally I believe God's Spirit is much too powerful for demonic forces to contend with. Paul reminds us in 1 Corinthians that we are the very temples where His Spirit abides. He goes on to say that God will destroy anyone who messes with His temple. (See 1 Corinthians 3:16-17) Scripture teaches that the demonic world is well aware of this truth. They shudder at the thought of invading God's turf. If Jay was indeed demon possessed it is because he was never born again. I'm not judging his salvation, I don't know what was in Jay's heart. I'm merely stating what the Bible teaches about demon possession.

Chapter 5

EIGHT LITTLE PIGTAILS

I must admit, I didn't care for Jay's brothers. Even Jay didn't care for Jay's brothers. Moreover, they all disliked him. By default, Jay's brothers despised me. But he ruled the roost so it didn't really matter to me what they thought. The only one Jay seemed to tolerate was his twelve-year-old sister, Roxanne. I remembered her well from grade school. She was a few years behind me and I am certain that she was the only black girl at the time at Kester Elementary. In a swarm of little whities she stood out like a forlorn freckle. I would often see her at recess hanging out in the playground area. Everything was different about this child from her mocha skin to the way she dressed and the eight curly pigtails which sprang from her ball-shaped head. As the only black girl on campus Roxanne got picked on often and didn't have many friends. So, I became her friend.

Though we were three years apart the span between us didn't seem all that great, at least from my juvenile perspective. I was a fifteen year old trapped in a twelve-year-old body and she, vice-versa. Puberty hit me late. I didn't earn the nickname Mouse because I had a deep baritone voice, quite the contrary. Your man here sounded like Felix the Cat after he'd been neutered. I had a baby face and scrawny legs, and I could grow about as much peach fuzz as a gecko lizard. For these reasons girls my own age scared the dickens out of me. They were blossoming into little women while I was still holding a magnifying glass to my armpits searching frantically for any remote evidence of manhood. Because I was biologically challenged with respect to puberty, I was much more comfortable with Roxanne than with the teenage girls in my own grade level.

While Jay was busy at work I would hang back at the Gowers' with Roxanne. This became our daily routine. Jay preferred it that way as he generally expected me there when he got home. So after school Roxanne and I both reported to the same household where we spent afternoons in Jay's bedroom. Mostly we'd just watched TV together.

I'm truly convinced we saw every rerun of the 'I Love Lucy' show from atop the same carpet floor. If Roxanne wasn't laughing at Fred or Ethel she was chuckling at my sorry impersonation of Ricky Ricardo. We also enjoyed watching that stone-age family, *The Flintstones*. I think we viewed every single episode of that cartoon series as well. If we had anything in common at all, it was an appreciation for lame cartoons. My dream as a youth was to do voiceovers for animated characters, funny characters like Barney Rubble. Pardon my boasting but I could imitate him pretty well. (*Ah-hih-hih, ah-hih-hih... ah sorry, Fred!"*) Roxanne would always bust up at my lame impersonations. The poor girl would typically cover her mouth when she laughed as her teeth were so buck, she could have chucked wood with them.

Roxanne was a petite thing but what she lacked in weight and size she made up in temper. The mirror would fall victim to many verbal lashings when Roxanne attempted to fix her hair. Her 'fro preferred all the way up but she always wanted to flatten it down. You would think she was fighting a Tasmanian devil if you ever heard her trying to tame those kinky locks of hers. She'd curse and scream and throw her brush down. It got ugly. Grooming usually set her off in a pretty foul mood and she'd require a good hour to cool down from her frenzied fit. All her fussing would be for nothing, though. The 'fro claimed its victory every time. She never should have gotten away from the eight little pigtails.

As our relationship blossomed Jay encouraged me to ask Roxanne to 'go steady.' The idea sounded very reasonable from my standpoint. After all we had *The Flintstones* in common and there is no truer test of compatibility than watching cartoons together. But to my dismay, when I popped the question she turned down my proposal as if I were Barney Rubble offering her pterodactyl soup. I didn't really care. It wasn't my idea anyway. So things continued on as they always had, hanging out in Jay's bedroom and having a *yabba-dabba-doo time* watching Fred and Barney together. But before long, when Roxanne turned thirteen, she reconsidered my offer and became my steady girlfriend. That was fine with me as long as I didn't have to help manage her frizzy hair.

24

This may sound strange to some but I never thought of Roxanne as being black or me as being white. Nor did either of us ever think of our relationship in terms of being interracial. I say this because others, especially on my side of the family, freaked out when the two of us hooked up. Some thought I was sure to put Grandpa in an early grave. It actually took me by surprise that this was an issue. Looking back I can see how our ages would have been of concern but pigmentation? My mother even took me to get counsel at the Baptist Church. A sweet old reverend listened quietly to Mom's concerns and patiently nodded his sleepy head. But he really didn't offer much advice. All I remember him saying was, "She's kinda' young." Yes, he was quite an observant old fella' with a knack for pointing out the obvious, like the mechanic who spends an hour under the hood of your car only to say, "By golly, there's a motor in there!"

The only one who got behind our relationship was Jay. Sad to say, he encouraged it to a fault. Jay would tell me things like, "You need to be holding her hand." or "You need to be kissing her." It got to a point where Jay was instructing me how these things were to be done. I thought this was normal, that it was for my benefit and that he was assuming the role of 'big brother'. I don't think Roxanne felt the need for this kind of affection anymore than I did. But Jay was much older and wiser so we cooperated. Though these intimate gestures were the product of third party manipulation they created a bond nonetheless. Roxanne and I got too involved way too early; emotionally and to a degree, physically. We were already two confused kids and this enforced physical intimacy made matters much worse.

It is not by coincidence that the following counsel is repeated in the Song of Solomon no less than three times; *"I charge you... do not stir up or awaken love until it pleases"* (SOS 2:7, 3:5 & 8:4) These words are not written to rip anyone off from something they might enjoy too much. They are not there because the Bible takes a position that sex is icky. On the contrary, you will find that God's Word places great value on intimacy within its proper context. Love, romance and sexual affection were created to be enjoyed by couples in a committed relationship. The warning in Song of Solomon is there to protect us from the problems, pressures, pitfalls and pain that come with intimacy outside of God's will.

I understand the dilemma for young people; their bodies are wired for what their emotions can't handle. In these poor defenseless vessels hormones are exploding like an overstuffed bag of microwave popcorn. I used this illustration at a youth camp recently. One of the youth pastors asked his group if they agreed with the 'popcorn' analogy. One twelve year old piped up, "I'm not even in the microwave yet!" One day he will be and on some occasions the control will be set to maximum power. That's when it's time to hit the off button. You either do that or you get burned and that's what the Lord wants to protect His kids from. While most teenagers don't have someone like Jay coaxing them into physical intimacy they are bombarded constantly by the media with sensual images and a message that says go for it. Job said, *"I have made an agreement with my eyes. Then how can I look with lust at a virgin?"* (See Job 31:1). If this married patriarch was so careful not to turn up the heat, how much more relevant are his words for those whose hormones are raging?

Chapter 6

FROM QUEER TO ETERNITY

While things continued to grow increasingly bizarre in my personal life, church life was just starting to make sense. My involvement at First Baptist quickly led to church service. (If you've ever been a Baptist you know the drill. You got to serve!) Again, it wasn't my idea but it didn't sound like a bad one. So I plugged in with the forth grade Sunday school class. Sunday school was held in the Bennet Building, named after the Bennet's who funded it of course. I actually knew the Bennet family back when I was a little tyke. They also bankrolled my father's campaign when he ran for congress. It was shortly after this unsuccessful attempt that he and my mom divorced. I never saw the Bennet's after that but it was a privilege to serve in a building named in their honor. At least something they contributed toward proved to be a worthy investment.

My duties in the Sunday school room were quite simple. Essentially, I handed out pencils, paper, crayons, hymnals, Sunday school lessons, basically everything but cigarettes and matches. It was about as exciting as watching a hubcap rust but I remained true to my calling. The teacher could always count on me to show up promptly, keep quiet and fulfill my tasks no matter how tedious. I wouldn't even giggle at the old geezers who strained their aged pipes to lead ancient hymns, even though they hit more sour notes than a box of Lemon Heads. The job was a no-brainer and I was uniquely qualified.

Everything was going hunky-dory until one day, without any warning my Christian service came to an abrupt end. I didn't even see it coming. The director of the children's department, a crotchety old sourpuss I'd never met before, intercepted me on my way to the classroom. This man was nothing like Reverend Harrah or Ric Wonders or Jim Allison. Not in the least. He was a real booger. "What is this I hear about you and Jay?" Mr. Kelp snapped while looking down his nose. I didn't have the slightest clue as to what he meant and wasn't exactly sure how to respond. "What's this I hear about you and Jay?" he barked again. I was not privy to the rumor mill he subscribed to and he had no idea what he was talking about. "I don't know." was the best I could come up with. "Is it true," Mr. Kelp sneered as if he had personally caught one of the FBI's ten most wanted, "that you and Jay are homosexuals?"

I was totally horrified that anyone would make such an accusation about us. After all, I was sweet on Jay's little sister. But I wasn't going to admit that to Mr. Kelp. Certainly he would see a teenage crush as some kind of federal offense as well. "No!" I shot back as I felt blood rush to my humiliated face. "Well, that's what I hear!" he retorted. I did all I could to defend my innocence but Mr. Kelp wasn't interested in anything I had to say for myself. "That's what folks are saying," he insisted. "So, it's best if you not serve in Sunday school class anymore." Any thoughts I may have had of Mr. Kelp presenting me with a congratulatory gold watch quickly vanished. My private little, Salem witch trial ended with me getting my walking papers.

Sad to say, I was dismissed from ministry at the ripe old age of fifteen because gossip didn't swing in my favor. Of all people, me! A kid!!! I was too naïve to even understand the gay lifestyle. But Mr. Kelp had convicted me and declared me guilty as charged. It didn't feel good. I had been branded and the iron stung. Not that I would ever miss handing out pencils but, did it have to end like this? I never really expected to get the boot after three months of faithful service. Not on a false homo rap!

28

This doesn't do much for a kid's self-esteem, and I didn't have much to begin with. I was determined then and there to check out of church altogether. However, my mom advised me to persevere and prove my accusers wrong. Honestly, that was my only incentive for staying at the First Baptist Church for as long as I did. I'd make a point of greeting Mr. Kelp with a big smile when I saw him but he'd just scowl. My attempts to sway his opinion failed. Maybe it was my soprano voice that threw him off.

There is a horrifying twist to this whole tragic tale though. Mr. Kelp and his informants were half-right in their allegation. They were wrong about me entirely but their suspicions about Jay were valid. I would discover this much later, the hard way, the hurtful way. He was a predator and I became his next victim. Sad to say, I might have been spared one of life's most painful tragedies had leadership taken a position to rescue me rather than condemn me. For this I resented the church and eventually turned my back on Christianity altogether. I dove headlong into a world which eagerly awaited hurt and troubled kids.

It is not my intent to blame Jay or Mr. Kelp for the decision I made to turn my back on Christ. Others have suffered worse fate and remained true to the Lord. Joseph was sold out by his brothers into slavery but not even that shook his faith. And though he wasn't a slave by choice he resolved to be the best slave he could be so God would be honored. Later in life Joseph was falsely accused of rape and thrown into the slammer. Yet he was determined to honor God by being a model prisoner. So how is it that guys like Joseph press further into God when bad things happen and guys like a young Terry Michaels get pushed further back? Is it the difference between maturity and immaturity? Or is this the difference between someone who is truly saved and someone that never was? Honestly, I think trying to answer that question gets real sticky for us Christians. I'm not sure God wants us in a place where we are making that kind of call. Judging the salvation of another is not our place. What the young Terry Michaels needed was grace not a label he could be pigeonholed with. I think this is a safe posture either way you look at it. When in doubt the best response is always grace, simply share the love of Jesus.

My experience of false accusations and rejection in the church has helped me see the wisdom of always following the scriptures. We read in Paul's epistle to the Galatians, *"Brothers and sisters, if a person gets trapped by wrongdoing, those of you who are spiritual should help that person turn away from doing wrong. Do it in a gentle way. At the same time watch yourself so that you also are not tempted."* (See Galatians 6:1) The principle here is restoration not condemnation. It is done in a spirit of humility not arrogance. Jesus also outlined the process of confronting a fallen brother when he said, *"If a believer does something wrong, go, confront him when the two of you are alone. If he listens to you, you have won back that believer. But if he does not listen, take one or two others with you so that every accusation may be verified by two or three witnesses."* I've often wondered what grief I may have been spared had Mr. Kelp followed these biblical precepts instead of following his human inclination to believe the worst.

Chapter 7

THE DEACON AND THE SALESMAN
Lessons from Chapter 6

Howard was your average guy. He lived in an average home in an average neighborhood. He had an average sized family: one wife, two kids and a dog named Sport. On an average month Howard earned an average income. Some months were better than average, others not. It all depended on how many used cars Howard sold on a monthly average, based of course on the average commission of his average sales. On those rare occasions when Howard sold more than average he would also drink more than average. "I hit the mother lode!" Howard would boast to his belching beer buddies at Buster's Bar.

Without exception Howard would always sit on the same old wobbly bar stool in the smoke filled tavern. He would drink an average of six and one half beers. He never really knew if it was the seventh beer that made him wobbly or if it was just the stool. So he rarely finished that last drink, even though it was usually a light beer. When the room got too wobbly for Howard he knew it was time to go home to his wife Marge. But poor Howard's return home was much later than average and Marge would assail him with angry words. But all was forgiven when Marge learned of the mother lode.

Howard believed there is an art to selling used cars. He had the art down to a science or maybe he had the science down to an art. Whichever it was he knew that he had the gift, at least on some rare occasions. Not only was it an art, not only was it a science, car sales was a game, a game that Howard enjoyed because he wrote his own rules. One rule was called 'con the consumer.' Another was 'lock the looker'. It was a game of wit over wallet. "Put 'em behind the wheel, make 'em think they gotta' deal!" is how he explained it to Marge. Howard was especially cunning when elderly ladies visited his lot. They were quite easy to outwit and could not detect your average auto malfunctions.

Howard was unashamed of his deceitful antics. He explained to Marge deception was necessary in order to make a decent living selling used autos. But he never referred to the cars on his lot as 'used autos' to his customers, he called them "pre-owned vehicles." According to Howard, that made them much more marketable.

Things got even more interesting once Howard lured his prey into the sales office. Once the customer was trapped in his lair Howard knew the odds were well in his favor. To the inevitable counter offers, Howard's response was always the same: "Well, I don't know if the sales manager will agree to your proposal. That's about what we paid for it but I'll see what he says." In reality there was no sales manager on this particular lot. Howard would simply disappear into a back room, light up a cigarette and sip some coffee. Then he would return to the office and tell the dupe, "The best we can do is..." and he'd pull some dollar amount out of the air. It was all part of the game.

At work Howard generally wore a bright plaid jacket with shiny white shoes and ties that seldom matched. It was his understanding that this was what your average used car salesman wore. Being the traditional sort Howard would declare with a grin, "I must follow suit." It was a humorous pun that always gave Marge quite a chuckle.

The average work schedule for Howard was Tuesday through Sunday and he always arrived on the lot at nine o'clock sharp.

Every Sunday morning he would stand in the driveway, wearing his plaid jacket and mismatched tie, and watch the cars zoom by. He always kept an eye out for Chet who drove the fancy red convertible sports coupe. Howard didn't know Chet personally but was very familiar with him because Chet once ran for public office. Howard wished he had a pre-owned vehicle like Chet's but couldn't afford such a luxury. He'd really have to hit a big mother lode for that to happen. But that was only a dream.

Unlike Howard, Chet was affluent and respectable. He didn't earn his wealth through dishonest gain. Chet graduated from university with top honors and climbed the corporate ladder in a dignified fashion. After much success in commercial advertising he became vice president of the corporation. Chet was not only successful in business he had earned a great reputation as a model citizen. He involved himself in community service and earned the title of Head Deacon at The First Community Church, which was just down the road from the car lot. Howard couldn't remember a Sunday he didn't see Chet pass by on his way to church. Chet was a very religious man to be sure.

The First Community Church was known for having the finest pipe organ in the state. Its pipes were many and some almost reached to the ceiling above the second story balcony. Everyone was well aware that Chet had donated the funds for its purchase. There was also a nice shiny bronze plaque with Chet's name on it positioned above the water fountain which he had donated. He had also helped finance the fellowship hall and the youth wing. Chet was very generous with his wealth. Often he was called upon to offer the benediction for Sunday services. On Tuesdays he hosted a men's prayer breakfast. It was well attended because Chet was well liked and very popular.

One Sunday morning Howard arrived at work with a slamming

headache. He attributed it to the beer he had at Busters Bar the night before but he did not offer that bit of information to his boss. Howard was excused for the day so he could nurse his ailing noggin. On the way home Howard noticed Chet's fancy red sports coupe parked in front of The First Community Church. He saw many other cars parked there as well, some new, some pre owned. Being the curious man he was Howard decided to venture inside. He found a seat in the back pew; it also had a plaque mounted on it with Chet's name. Howard quickly noticed Chet seated in the very front row.

Minister Mike offered a moving message. He talked about a rich young ruler who came running to Jesus. The young ruler asked Jesus, "What must I do to inherit eternal life?" This struck a chord with Howard as he had been thinking about that very question a great deal in recent days. Minister Mike talked about the importance of following Christ. He went on to say that the rich young ruler went away very sad because he didn't want to follow Jesus. This disturbed Howard greatly, he did not want to leave sad.

At the close of the service the church began to empty but Howard remained. Even after the entire congregation had left Howard stayed seated. The words of Minister Mike echoed in his ears and resonated into his heart. He sat there long and quietly as if glued to the pew. The only other person in the building was Chet. He had stayed late to polish the plaque above the water fountain. As he rubbed away at the bronze Chet began to think of all the great things he had done for First Community Church; how he had donated funds for the pipe organ, youth wing and fellowship hall, and how he led a well attended prayer breakfast for the men on Tuesday mornings. Thinking on these things Chet was led to go into the sanctuary and offer a little prayer which went something like this:

"Thank you, Lord, that my life has significance. I praise Thee that I am charitable and that everyone at the First Community Church benefits from my generosity. I give thanks unto thee that the men in this church are praying men as a result of my affective leadership on Tuesday mornings. Lord, you knoweth that thy people worship because of the magnificent organ which I donated. I was happy to do this for You, God. Oh, and P.S. I'm so glad I'm not like that sleazy used car salesman in the plaid jacket that doth stink up thy very pew I donate-eth. Amen."

Fortunately, Howard did not hear Chet's prayer. He was too engrossed in his own. Falling to his knees and with tears streaming down his cheeks Howard cried, "Forgive me, Lord, I'm a rotten scoundrel!" Howard left the First Community Church whistling to the tune of *Amazing Grace*. And he never wore his plaid jacket again.

Based upon the parable of the Pharisee and the
Publican
Luke 18:10-14

Chapter 8

ARE YOU RUNNING WITH ME, JESUS?

Have you ever wondered how the people of your past might remember you? Journaling my life forces me to think on such things. I suppose that can be a pleasant experience for some people. Looking back on my own sordid youth I hope that most of my footsteps have been graciously erased by the kindness of time. Mostly, I hope the mark I left was too insignificant to file away in anybody's grey matter. I have no academic achievements to boast of, no athletic accomplishments, no trophies or awards, no student body titles, just a lowly spot on some wretched school bench that quietly whispers I was there. But even that mark will have been faded by the more lasting impression of bird droppings. If anyone were to remember me, they would surely be mindful of all my shameful baggage. I carried a lot of it. That's much of who I was and how I would be remembered by most of my teachers and classmates. The unfortunate thing about being a troubled kid is the stigma attached. I was not only known as 'troubled' but was labeled as 'trouble' and ill repute seemed to tag along with me wherever I went. Yet today I serve an awesome God who redeems the years which the canker worm and locust have stolen.

*   *   *   *   *

I don't blame people for not liking me, I didn't like me either. There were kids I hung out with but none I considered to be soul mates. We were all misfits and most of us didn't even like each other. The common denominator in my clique was Jimmy Van Patten. We all liked him and I think it is safe to say he liked most of us. But most of us didn't like anybody but Jimmy.

Though Jimmy wasn't tight with a lot of people he was well known on campus. His dad was a popular character actor on both the big and small screen who went on to star as the father in the popular sitcom called 'Eight is Enough.' Jimmy was also getting small acting parts at the time but nothing like his younger brother, Vincent, who was scoring some major roles in Disney films. When I knew them the Van Patten's all resided in a luxurious townhouse community in Sherman Oaks called Horace Heights. Horace Heights was a sanctuary for exotic birds and rich people. Throughout the grounds there were brooks flowing amidst lush foliage. Dozens of giant birdcages teemed with a host of noisy, feathered creatures.

Another member of our campus clan was Bill. He also lived in Horace Heights. Bill and I never really got along. Actually, I hated his guts and he hated mine. Bill was this short redheaded dumpling and his mouth was a fountain of insults, just spewing all the time. We were always getting into tangles because I couldn't stand his mouthing off at me. One time I shut his yap with my fist. I didn't think he'd punch me back but he walloped me one and bloodied my lip pretty good. He didn't mouth off at me much after that incident but I still didn't like the twerp. We just kind of tolerated each other because we both hung around Jimmy.

Dennis was a different story, I did sort of like him. He was a blonde haired Swede who lived in the Barrio. Though this chunky kid grew up in Sweden he was convinced he was a Chicano. He spoke with a broken Euro-Mexican accent and always confused his English with Spanish. Dennis preferred to dress like a Mexican lowrider and sported the pointy black shoes we called "cockroach killers".

I never got to know most of the kids in our clique outside of school. I can't even tell you where they lived. There was Kinsey who rarely spoke a word. I'm not sure anyone in our clan ever had a real conversation with the guy. He just sat there like a porch dog and smiled occasionally if someone said something amusing. Then there was Zack and John and Dave. We all hung out in the quad together at lunchtime but when the bell rang, we all became sudden strangers disappearing into our undisclosed locations. This went on for years, junior high and high school, hanging with the same crowd but never discovering the secret lives they led off campus. With the exception of Dennis and Bill, I didn't know which dwelt among the privileged or lived in the slums. All I cared about was where Jimmy lived. I logged many hours at Horace Heights and Jimmy put in a lot of time at my humble home. For all I know the rest of the guys could have been trolls that slept under a bridge somewhere.

Jimmy had come to California from Queens and he spoke with a funny New York accent, like Rodney Dangerfield on crack. His voice was always filled with enthusiasm as if Ed McMahon had just arrived at his door to announce that he had won the Publisher's Clearing House sweepstakes. His huge blue eyes were always lit up as if he really was celebrating some kind of big win. Life always seemed a surprise to him in vivid contrast to me. I had the countenance of one who just had a cop show up at my door with a warrant. Initially I thought Jimmy was kind of odd. He was into these stupid magic tricks and he played a lot of practical jokes... mean practical jokes which at times were played on me.

I think I was the first kid to befriend Jimmy when he moved to the San Fernando Valley from Hollywood Hills but I am also willing to concede that my recollection is somewhat fuzzy. I offer this disclaimer as there is an old saying - if you can remember the sixties you probably weren't there. Having done the math, however, I think it's likely that I was there. I'm further convinced I was Jimmy's first friend. Speaking of math, that is exactly how Jimmy and I met. He sat behind me in math class.

It was a class for kids who didn't get math. Jimmy and I were much more advanced than that; I'm not sure how we wound up in there. Most likely it had to do with overcrowding in the Los Angeles County school district. In our jurisdiction any electives requested were automatically forwarded to the *Make a Wish Foundation*. As far as the three 'R's, unless you were an honor student they'd stick you anywhere. The classes were always packed tighter than a can jammed with Playdoh. In beginner's arithmetic Jimmy and I were gifted students. Because of our superior skills in basic addition and subtraction we always finished our work rather quickly, so we felt justified when we dragged into class late, breezed through our assignments then spent the rest of the period goofing off or, as Mr. Brown put it, disrupting everybody. Grades were never a problem for Jimmy or me in Mr. Brown's class. We managed to get A's on all our work. I'm not bragging mind you, any third grader would have scored well. But because Jimmy and I were such goof-offs Mr. Brown failed us after the first semester. This came as quite a shock not only to us but also to our parents.

I am quite certain that Jimmy and I set a new precedent for Van Nuys Junior High School that year. We were the first kids in history to receive a failing grade from Mr. Brown. Up until 1969 most believed this to be virtually impossible. Though we proved both the entire faculty and student body wrong I was not proud of our accomplishment. I was destined to change the course of history once again by raising my score from a flunk to an A by the following semester, which I did. I am not sure how Jimmy fared the second time around but I was not too worried for him. Being the magician he was he could easily turn an F to an A with the stroke of a wand... as long as it had ink in it.

One time Jimmy brought a long stick to class. I didn't know exactly why and didn't care to ask. Thinking back I probably should have. My assumption was he had another stupid trick up his paisley sleeve. Before long Jimmy had me raising my right hand with my fingers curled into a circle as if holding onto a pipe. Then he told me to look to the front of the class and like a complete jackass I did. That's when he slid the long sharp stick through my hand and jabbed Kurt, who was seated directly in front of me. Kurt let out a loud yelp. By the time he turned around Jimmy had let go of the suspicious spear and I was looking guilty as all heck, at least from Kurt's perspective. I'm telling you, the kid had fire in his eyes and was flaming mad. I declined his offer to meet him at the bike racks after school as I didn't want my butt kicked for something I didn't do.

Jimmy was the first close friend I ever had that came from a happy and healthy two-parent home. All my other pals prior to him had either been stung by divorce or placed into foster families. In contrast, Jimmy had a loving mom and a very involved dad and two brothers he was super tight with. The oldest, Nels, didn't pounce on Jimmy and Jimmy never beat up on Vincent. They were all best buddies. I always admired how they all got along so well. It was obvious that they had tremendous affection for one another. They were much like the TV family in 'Eight is Enough' only with five less kids. Though I was a troubled boy the Van Patten clan gave me a sense of self worth because they were generally very kind and affirming toward me.

I brought Jimmy with me to the Mustard Seed many times and we talked a lot about faith. He was definitely a believer but I don't know if I'd go so far as to call him a follower. At least he wasn't hypocritical about this, he was who he was. I also owe it to Jimmy for buying me my first Christian book. It was a compilation of prayers called 'Are You Running with Me, Jesus?' As I look back upon my life I know He was, even when I was crawling.

Chapter 9

MY SECOND TIME DRUNK

I was with Jimmy the second time I got drunk, and I'm pretty sure it was his first. My first time was quite by accident. It began with the girl next door daring me to eat chili peppers. After frying my gullet with nature's wicked spices she got into her parents liquor and poured me some nasty chasers. The little vixen brought out all kinds of unidentified fluids then challenged me to chug the stuff down. I only remember these concoctions tasting like kerosene as they ate their way down my tender throat with the fury of Hell's fire. But as any brave, twelve year old trooper would do, I took it like a man. The last thing I remember was waking up on my front lawn hours later. I crawled into my house then into bed where I slept an entire day away. My first time drunk also led to my first ever hangover. I remember staring at my own green reflection in toilet water as I spouted off like a seasick beluga. I never wanted to drink again after that but Jimmy convinced me otherwise.

We stood anxiously in front of the shady liquor store on the boulevard. There the two of us waited for the perfect stranger to arrive onto the scene, one who'd be willing to help us in our mischievous errand. We kept our eyes out for anyone with that tell-tell look, an appearance of being non-threatening, compliant and sympathetic to the cause of teenaged wine bibbers. Anyone sophisticated or conservative or mature looking need not apply. Naturally, this ruled out any old geezers with gray or white hair or shiny baldheads. Slacks and blazers was also a deal breaker. This was a job that required somebody young and hip. Long hair, facial whiskers and worn out bell bottoms would identify the chosen one for us. After awhile the ideal candidate caught our attention. A shaggy hippy drifted out from the icehouse with his hippy-chick girlfriend clutched close to his side. They met our most crucial criteria: hip and over twenty-one, but not over thirty. "Can you get some wine for us?" Jimmy begged with eyes drooping like a love-starved basset hound. Our new hippy friends were more than eager to oblige us. However, they thought it might look a little conspicuous if they went back inside the liquor store for a second purchase especially after being seen talking to a couple of suspicious fourteen year olds. But our bushy partner in crime had a plan. Jimmy and I got into the backseat of his rusty old heap and we headed off to the market up the boulevard.

Our hairy pal rolled in front of the store then held out his hand over the tattered car bench. I thought he was giving me five, you know, the ol' hippy handshake, so I slapped his palm with mine. "No, the money!" he quickly corrected me. Feeling like a complete idiot I handed him the cash. Once our flower children chauffeurs disappeared into the market Jimmy broke into total hysterics. He continued laughing and repeating, "No, the money!" After about ten straight minutes of Jimmy busting his gut our hippy friends finally returned to the beat up rattrap we were sitting in. They climbed up front and presented us with an odd green bottle which resembled an overgrown gourd. It had a large round base with a long narrow neck and on the label it said *Spanada* in big happy letters. I knew this was quality stuff when I didn't get change back for my two dollars. After doing our evil bidding the kind couple drove us to Sherman Oaks Park so Jimmy and I could offer a toast to peace, love and all that is groovy. We found a patch of grass to sit on then quickly unscrewed the cap and shared the Hawaiian Punch of fine cabernets. The only thing missing were candles and Englebert Humperdink crooning on the transistor radio. We sipped into the evening's twilight until we were left with a lukewarm blend of sangria and backwash swirling at the bottom of our pretty glass gourd. And all night long Jimmy kept repeating, *"No, the money!"* Then he'd break out into utter hysterics.

The hour was getting late and the sky was growing dark and eerie. With a half bottle of Spanada sloshing around in each of our considerably small bellies, Jimmy and I decided to roam the dim lit park. That's when we ran into a couple of girls from school. Neither Jimmy nor I had ever met them before but were very aware of their reputations. These were the girls moms warned their sons about. For one, they dressed extremely daring. The ultra-revealing outfits they typically wore did not appear to be a show of sensuality. There was a darker side to it. It seemed to be a blatant act of defiance, a statement against social norms. Unless one had a dark side it did more to repel lookers that to attract them. I'm reminded of a popular folksong of our day by Crosby, Stills, Nash and Young called, 'Teach Your Children.' There is a line in that tune which states, "You... who are on the road... must have a code... that you can live by!" I would never suggest that CSN&Y should be considered poster boys for standards and values but even they promoted ideals that were widely embraced by the mainstream of secular society. The risqué style of Lisa and Diane led many kids to believe they had no code to live by. Furthermore, it appeared as if they were retaliating against any established codes of public decency. Any person with a heart of God would have wept for these two girls. They could not have advertised any more plainly that their souls were in desperate need of salvation. But that's not how Jimmy and I saw things at the time. From our perspective, these were the kind of girls to run from.

If their fashion statement wasn't shocking enough, they were also said to be witches. Just the kind of gals you want to run into late at night in the dark! These juvenile broom jockeys, Lisa and Diane, soon introduced us to an even drearier kind of darkness, one which we really had no interest in. It actually haunted us.

45

They each explained how both their mom's taught them from an early age the art of witchcraft and how to cast spells and even mentioned names of people at school they had pronounced curses upon. Some were teachers; others were classmates we both knew. They'd pluck hair out of their unsuspecting heads then use it in their efforts to cause harm. If that wasn't creepy enough we were totally freaked out when these wayward witches presented their 'statement of faith'; it was anti-faith and anti-Christ in the most literal sense.

Just as I had remembered Stan Angel sharing 'light' the young Elvira's shared 'darkness' with Jimmy and me under the eerie shadows of a moonlit sky. I didn't know it at the time but Satan worshippers have a gospel message of their own. It is one they even consider to be good news but to the discerning it is as damning as it is blasphemous. Lisa told us that Jesus was actually a son of Satan. She went on to tell us that God was so jealous of the devil that He went on a mad campaign to convince the world that Christ was really His son. Then she advocated the idea that God was using the false promise of eternal life as an attempt to lure people to follow Him. Now I don't know if all Satanists believe this garbage about Jesus or if it is just some twisted lie propagated by some. All I know is that it was quite frightening and extremely disturbing to a junior higher intoxicated with sangria.

Even though I was fully backslidden by this time God clearly had His hand upon me. As I listened to Lisa and Diane carry on with all their satanic mumbo-jumbo I sensed the presence of something, no, *Someone* more powerful than darkness. Though I was not at a place in my life where I was seeking righteousness, I surely didn't want any of this sewage. I didn't buy it. It stunk to high heaven and the good Lord would not allow me to have anything to do with it. He would allow me to toast the moonlight with a jug of Sangria and he would permit me to pass out in my own puke but no way was He handing off the pink slip to my soul. I was His whether I wanted to accept it at that moment or not.

Sometimes I think the greatest evidence for the existence of God is seeing what mankind is reduced to when God is subtracted from his life. I see what my life became when I walked away from the Lord and it literally haunts the hell out of me. I never want to go back to that place. And when I think of two fourteen year old girls worshipping evil as part of a family tradition it truly says something to me about the heart of fallen man. It's really quite horrifying. Such a depraved lifestyle bears undisputable testimony that there is an evil force at work in our world. I for one firmly confirm there is a counter-force that can overcome this dark power. Call me old fashioned if you will but I believe good still conquers evil. And I am convinced that there is a master creature behind the power of evil and a greater Master Creator behind all that is good. I also have come to understand that this Master Creator even loves lost little witches and gave His life for them that they might live.

Chapter 10

JOY RIDE
A Crash Course in Driving

We never planned on joy riding; it just happened. Sin is like that, isn't it? You don't ever have to go looking for it, it finds you. And unless you're willing to flee from sin, sin will claim you for its own. But sin is tricky. It does not force anything upon anyone. It woos you with thrills and adventure. It offers you the ride of a lifetime. But that ride inevitably results in a crash. Someone gets hurt. Someone pays. If not you then someone else and the cost is rarely cheap. That's the lesson I learned when Jimmy and I went for a joy ride.

The evening began innocently enough. We were on a religious pursuit if you will, walking to the Mustard Seed, minding our own business. Somehow we strayed off the path. It was Jimmy's idea but I followed him every step of the way. We were almost at our destination, no more than an eighth of a block away. But when we passed by the Magic Muffler parking lot we got other ideas. Once Jimmy set eyes upon all those shiny vehicles there was no stopping him. He had to look. He suggested I also come along. There were a variety of classics in the big lot, parked like pretty maids all in a row while resting in the shade of a hideous purple garage. Plus there were more besides in front of the auto restoration shop next door. Naturally we were curious. We'd both be in the market for a vehicle soon so it was imperative that we do a little preliminary research and find out which cars would best serve our needs.

The restoration shop offered a number of exquisite possibilities: vintage Rolls Royces, antique Bentleys and early model Jaguars that were fixed up like brand new. Each was showroom quality.

I'd never be able to afford such a luxury but Jimmy didn't rule out the idea. We opened them one by one. We smelled the leather interiors. We ran our hands over the velvety seats and felt around every contour of the smooth dashboards with our curious little fingers. We sat inside and tested for comfort and headroom. We inspected every last control, knob, button, handle and lever. Jimmy took inventory of all the high-end features. I checked everything mechanical: brakes, steering and mileage. Everything met our criteria for comfort, style and functionality. The only thing left to check was performance. So together, Jimmy and I went on a mad hunt for the keys. Yes, keys! You can't test performance without those little jobs can you? So we searched. I investigated the glove compartment while Jimmy checked behind the visors. We pulled up the car mats but they were not there. We scanned every crack and crevice but as hard as we searched we could not find one solitary key for the Rolls... or the Jag... or even the Bentley. Our hunt was not over though, not even by a long shot. It was decided we would lower our standards and venture over to where the inferior vehicles were parked. After all, we were mainly interested in transportation, something to get us from point A to point B. At fifteen status symbols can be compromised. We'd upgrade in a couple years when image mattered.

The muffler shop did offer a more modest selection of vehicles. They didn't smell of new leather, they bore the stench of old axle grease. And they lacked all those fine features of the models from the restoration shop. But they did have something the Rolls didn't have, or the Jag or the Bentley. You guessed it, they had keys! You're feeling the enthusiasm here, aren't you? We felt it too. After much deliberation Jimmy and I agreed upon the Datsun. It was newer than any of the luxury autos next door and had much less mileage. With four doors and child safety locks in the back it was also very practical. How could we go wrong?

Jimmy assumed the driver's seat and I took shotgun. Neither of us knew exactly how to drive but Jimmy had watched his dad work the controls many times before.

His inexperience stuck out like a purple muffler but Jimmy managed to crank up the ignition and shift gears into drive. Next thing I knew he was pulling out onto the boulevard. That's right, Van Nuys Boulevard! We were cruising! Well, semi cruising anyway. Jimmy was all over the road while I was wishing I had my 'Are You Running with Me, Jesus?' handbook to hold onto. It was a miracle we didn't get pulled over.

We had no intentions of stealing the Datsun, mind you. It was understood we would return it as soon as we were finished with our test drive. And that is exactly what we did do. We cautiously cruised down the seven mile stretch of Van Nuys Boulevard then drove straight back. When we returned to Magic Muffler I realized Jimmy had not paid enough attention to his dad's parking skills. He didn't miss the parking space by much. And had that Rolls Royce not been in the way I am quite certain he would have made it. But somehow the Datsun collided with that wonderfully restored vintage luxury automobile. Though this was a most unfortunate incident it did help me with my research. I noted for future reference that Rolls Royces fare much better in auto collisions than Datsuns.

The Rolls did indeed suffer minimal damage. Jimmy put a handsome crease in the right rear fender and a smashed tail light dangled sadly on a single wire. The Datsun didn't look so good. The entire front end was smashed up like an accordion after a drunken polka party. "Oh my gosh!" I exclaimed after the crash, "What do we do?" With eyes wide as hubcaps, Jimmy responded with one word, *"Run!!!"* And that is precisely what we did... all the way to the Mustard Seed. Alas, we were back on

51

track on our religious pursuit... praying we would never get caught for our dastardly deed. Many years later I would see the Van Patten clan on the infamous Mike Douglas Show. I remember the host asking Jimmy if he had ever gotten into big trouble. Without hesitation Jimmy answered, "No." For the most part, this is true. Neither of us ever got into trouble for our little joy ride. No one ever found out.

*   *   *   *   *

I recently read a story about the late, great preacher Dr. Donald Barnhouse. After delivering a sermon on the consequences of sin a young fellow told him that his conscience never ever bothered him. Dr. Barnhouse looked him in the eye and asked, "What would happen if I dropped an eight-hundred pound weight on a dead man? Would it bother him?" He explained to the young man that if sin didn't bother him it was most likely because he was dead.[2]

Though I was a sinner, apparently I was still alive. I never felt right about what happened at Magic Muffler. It didn't set well with my conscience to destroy property and just bail. So the next time Jimmy suggested joy riding I declined. But Jimmy told other kids about the opportunities available at the muffler shop. And those kids told their friends. Before long the Magic Muffler lot was surrounded by a tall chain link fence. Two salivating Doberman pinchers awaited anyone daring enough to climb over.

Sin does have a way of finding you and unless you flee from it things can get pretty messy. It's much like when someone throws

---

[2] Jon Courson's Application Commentary, Ephesians 4:19, page 1252

a rock into a mud puddle, there's that splatter affect where innocent bystanders take the hit. Sin also has a tendency to splatter on other people even though the real culprit may come out looking clean. That's the greatest tragedy of all; innocent parties are often the ones who pay the highest price while the offender seemingly gets off scot-free. That was certainly true in our case. My sin and Jimmy's didn't cost us anything, at least on the surface. But others sure paid dearly. The price tag on our joyride was the repair of a Rolls and a Datsun, the installation of a tall fence and the purchase of a couple Dobies. That's a hefty price to pay for two mischievous kids to cruise the boulevard.

The Bible is chock-full of testimonials which attest to the splattering affects of sin. One good example is Abraham. God promised this old codger that he and his barren wife, Sarah, would have a son together. But, as time wore on, the anxious couple grew increasingly impatient. Sarah's maid, Hagar, was soon introduced into the picture to ease their frustrations. The result was Ishmael and his offspring. The Old Testament records a long and painful history of God's chosen people and how they suffered at the hands of the sons of Ishmael. Even today the repercussions of Abraham's blunder are felt worldwide. What happened in a small tent has splattered our entire globe. But it won't be long before the true Promised Son cleans it all up for good.

Chapter 11

SEE YOU AT THE MOVIES

We didn't have multi-screen cinemas when I grew up. We had walk-in theatres: one ticket booth, one screen, and one concession stand, one per town. There was the Capri in Van Nuys, the La Reina in Sherman Oaks and the Reseda Walk-in in downtown Reseda. There were a host of others in the San Fernando Valley but the general rule was one per town. They all looked identical. They had the same red velour seats, and they all smelled of stale buttered popcorn. The only thing that set one apart from another was what they showed on the big screen. Naturally, we didn't have web sites we could visit to see what was playing. Nor could you drive downtown and read a list of options off a large marquee. The simplest way to find out what was showing was to open the entertainment section of *The Valley News and Green Sheet*, and you hoped that something decent was playing nearby.

I always knew what was showing at the Capri because it was on the boulevard and I passed by it practically everyday. When *The Sound of Music* came to town it stayed at the Capri for months. They lost my business during that time. I did come back for the hip and tragic biker tale of *Easy Rider* though. It ended with a crash and so did Peter Fonda's career. But *Easy Rider* was pivotal in launching Jack Nicholson to stardom. Rumor had it that the Capri was shutting down when 'The Last Picture Show' was displayed on the marquee. We were all relieved to discover that this was only a movie title. It was a scandalous film starring Timothy Bottoms and a significantly less wrinkled Cloris Leachman. (Bless her heart.)

Though there was usually one theatre per town you could always count on a double feature wherever you went. It was much like going to a rock concert where you'd have an opening act before the featured band played. Usually the opening act was some second rate pop group whose prior gig was at the local bowling alley. Then the headliner would come out and help you forget what you just suffered through by delivering a first class show. That's how it was at the movies. There was normally some cheesy B flick defiling the screen just prior to the main attraction. That was always a good time to visit the concession stand and stock up snacks for the feature presentation. When my mom took Rick and me to see *Butch Cassidy and the Sundance Kid* we had to tolerate this hideous film entitled *The Prime of Miss Jean Brody*. That was way too excruciating for two teenage boys to endure. It got even more awkward during the scene where this unwholesome gal posed for a nude portrait. The scene seemed to last forty-five minutes or so, especially since we were sitting next to my mom, who had the innocence of a nun.

We also had a drive-in theatre in Van Nuys. I think the rule for drive-ins was one per every ten towns. Lucky for me, though, the Sepulveda Drive-In was right near my house. I saw quite a few features there but they were all silent movies. They were silent because I watched them from the parking lot next door. I'd sit on the narrow seat of my ten-speed Huffy and preview what was playing until an angry store manager would run me off. While I rarely got to see a full-length feature from start to finish I did get to preview some very long movie trailers. But I'd be peddling away before I saw anyone on the big screen ride off into the sunset. However, there was at least one time I made it to the closing credits at the Sepulveda Drive-in without paying admission. It was when I saw *The Cowboys,* starring John Wayne.

Jay and I just happened to be walking down Sepulveda Boulevard one evening when Jimmy and Vincent drove by with their dad. Mr. Van Patten pulled up while Jimmy waved us over. "Wanna' go to the Drive-in?" he called with a cheery east coast inflection. Our hearts said yes but our wallets said, "You're outta' luck, dudes!" But, as a gesture of kindness and generosity, Mr. Van Patten offered to sneak us in. He popped open the spacious trunk of his late model Delta 88 Oldsmobile and we climbed aboard. "Don't make a peep!" he whispered as the huge steel lid fell toward our faces. By the time we crept out of our dark hole, Mr. Van Patten was stretching the canned speaker to the car window. Then we all sat back to watch *The Cowboys.*

Watching movies with the Van Patten's was like dining out with Food Network princess Rachel Ray. It wasn't just entertainment to them. It was part of their diet, the dessert they saved their fork for. They keep their eyes glued to the screen, taste every frame of the film, savor it then salivate for more. Mr. Van Patten was fascinated by *The Cowboys* and offered a colorful running commentary. "This is a fantastic movie!" he'd exclaim. "I'm really involved!" When I'm involved in a movie I tend to get lock jaw but not Mr. Van Patten. "Oh this is terrific!" he'd carry on. "Do you like it Jimmy?" I completely understood why Mr. Van Patten went into showbiz. It was more than a craft or some meaningless path to popularity for him; it was his lifeblood and passion. If I had been as passionate about Jesus as Mr. Van Patten was about film I never would have backslid.

*   *   *   *   *

When you're a fifteen year old with the face of a twelve year old it's hard to pass yourself off as a seventeen year old. I mention this to tell you I was restricted from seeing many movies, specifically the 'R' rated kind. With my baby face, lying about my age wasn't even an option. And a false ID was way too risky for a squeaky rascal like me. I'd get found out in a heartbeat. But there were 'R' rated movies I desperately wanted to see and I wasn't willing to sit through another one with my mother. I had to come up with something that would spare us both of that kind of embarrassment.

I finally found a way to beat the system and it worked like a charm every time; tinted glasses and a fake mustache. This wasn't one of those cheap mustaches you wear with some tacky, five-and dime Halloween costume. Mine was the kind professional actors wore in motion pictures. It was made of authentic human hair which was blonde just like my own. A sticky substance called spirit gum was used to glue the cookie duster beneath my schnozola. This simple disguise aged me by about two or three years, just enough to slip me under the puberty radar. I never got carded when I wore the 'stache. I think the ticket lady was actually too bewildered to card me. I probably looked like a total freak. I'm sure I sounded like one too when my Felix the Cat voice squeaked, "One ticket for *Barbarella* please."

If you've ever wondered what a hypocrite is I just described one for you. A hypocrite wears a disguise and pretends to be something he is not. Many Christians are often accused of being hypocrites because they are sinners but the truth is not all sinners are hypocrites. A hypocrite would be a Christian who hides the fact that he is a sinner. He pretends to be more spiritual than he actually is. If you can admit to being a sinner saved by grace, and you make a genuine attempt to be the same person on Monday that you are on Sunday, chances are you are not a hypocrite. But if the person on Sunday doesn't line up with the one on Monday, you've got a mask full of spirit gum... and that's when things get real sticky!

Chapter 12

THE SCREAM HEARD AROUND THE CORNER

My relationship with Jay lasted well over a year, maybe even two, I'm not really sure. It is a season in my life I try to block from my mind. These memories are just too repulsive and painful. The important thing is I got out. I wish I could say I escaped unscathed but this is not the case.

*   *   *   *   *

Jay became increasingly more demanding of my time. He needed me like a yo-yo needs string. He tried to convince me that with all his issues, insecurities and ailments he couldn't survive a solitary day without my personal intervention. Initially I bought into all this malarkey and felt sorry for him. So I was there for the guy. But it wasn't long before pity turned into resentment. And those demons! *Those disgusting demons!* They grew more aggressive and increasingly more perverted by the day. Eventually I grew very suspicious of these foul characters. Were they really evil spirits? (The Reverend Tom Fifer seemed to think so.) Or was Jay just plain schizo? Perhaps it was all just a big ploy! Could it be? Could Jay actually be that calculating, conniving and manipulative? It got to a point where I really didn't care whether it was demons or a sane Jay or an insane Jay or Sybil's lost twin. By this time, I was no longer concerned about saving him from the devil. I had had enough. I was checking out even if I was the only thing standing between Jay and Hell's fire. It was time to fight for my own life.

For so long I desperately tried to excuse Jay's demented behavior. But none of this helped me sleep at night. I would sob on my pillow in utter torment or just lay awake and silently mouth every curse word I knew. "Why me, God?" I'd scream in a soft whisper so as not to disturb Rick in the bed next to me. There was that feeling of wanting to puke but I couldn't. I needed someone to talk to, yet for fear of humiliation and shame I kept my agony hidden. The frustration I felt was so overwhelming at times I would even bust soda bottles over my head. But the only real damage I was left with was what Jay did to me.

I needed to break free, this was apparent; both my mental health and emotional stability depended upon it. But how? Jay had such control over my life. He controlled my time, my decisions, and my relationship with Roxanne. The monster controlled my every move! Should I fail to cooperate with him, he'd whimper like a big baby. He'd say things like, "You're not a true brother!" or he'd go into hysterics and throw an ugly tantrum. One time he put his fist through the living room window because I withstood him. Blood shot out of his wrist like Niagara Falls. Naturally this was perceived as my fault and Jay's brothers threatened to kill me for it. I didn't really care if they did, though. At least my troubles would be over.

Telling Jay to take a hike was not going to be easy, I knew this. There would certainly be hell to pay. And because Jay controlled my relationship with Roxanne I knew this relationship was on the line as well. Though I was not ready to break things off with her it was a risk I had to take. I could no longer live with myself if I didn't shake off Jay with all his psychotic imps. Once I had determined to do this I got pretty amp'd up for it. No longer would I be this timid, tender little Terry. Boldness would be my strongest ally.

I met with Jay at Sherman Oaks Park. Why not? His host of evil spirits could hook up with my witch pals Lisa and Diane and take a hike with them. We sat on a picnic table near Magnolia, the street leading to Horace Heights which was less than a couple blocks away. It was then and there I told Jay I wanted nothing more to do with him. Perhaps I should have explained why but I didn't. The truth is I couldn't. I was still trying to process everything, search the back of my mind for one last excuse for his sick behavior, avoid a tantrum, I don't know... I was scared. He even asked me, "Is it because you think I'm queer?" A yes would have only opened a can of worms; I wasn't ready to go there. I just wanted to tell Jay to hit the road and be done with it. I didn't want to hang in a dark park after all he had put me through and debate his sexual orientation. Nor did I care to suffer his wrath if he didn't like my answer. "No," I nervously muttered, but inside I was screaming a big 'YES!' That's what I really wanted to say. But I didn't. I just told him, *"Git!"* and left it at that.

Jay insisted on answers and explanations but I wasn't offering any. I didn't want to hear his excuses nor was I concerned about the tears flooding from his livid, angry face. There was nothing he could say or do to alter my decision. Finally Jay grew so frustrated he began yelling at the top of his lungs. He yelled louder than I had ever heard him yell before. He yelled louder than I had ever heard anyone yell before in my entire life. *"TERRY!!!"* he roared. *"HOW CAN YOU DO THIS TO ME?"* This should have been my question for him after I had caught onto all his perverse antics. The nerve that he would even ask me! I didn't answer. He yelled the question in various forms over and over again while I just shook my head in disbelief. That was the last time we spoke.

When I saw Jimmy at school the following day he asked me, "What happened with you and Jay last night?" Trying to play stupid I replied, "What do you mean?" Jimmy had heard Jay screaming all the way from Horace Heights. I felt utterly humiliated. I didn't know how to respond. But there was no dodging the question. "I told Jay to stay away from me!" Jimmy's huge blue eyes widened with wonder. He kept repeating, "He sounded like you were breaking up with him." I'm thinking under my breath, "You don't get it do you? I was a hostage! I finally broke loose from the creep and he freaked." But there was no way to explain things without looking like a total jackass. I just let his comment go.

Though I was finally free from Jay's evil grip I was not completely delivered from all the agony and pain. I continued to lay awake at night sick to my stomach while sobbing like a baby. The truth was, I did feel like a total jackass, like there was something I could have done to prevent what had happened. This is quite common among victims of molestation. You feel suckered into something so dirty and so debased but lack the sense to stop it. I suppose many kids my age would have caught on and retaliated. I didn't and that was a hard thing to live with. Now I know better. I know how perpetrators like Jay operate. They work relentlessly to earn your loyalty and love. Whatever you're missing in life they become; that dad, that big brother, that best friend, whatever. Co-dependencies develop and you are led to believe that a needy relationship between two males is actually a healthy thing. Then there are the gifts and all the kind gestures and trips to the amusement park. If they can't take you to *Neverland* they bring it to you. Then come the lies, "This is how real brothers show affection." or "The demon made me do it." Usually by this time the bonds are so tight you're convinced the prince can do no wrong. In your brainwashed mind he's been placed on the highest pedestal imaginable. He's your hero, savior and dearest pal. Yet it's all a game, a game predators play so well. They are calculating and conniving and don't care about whose life they might ruin in their depraved quests.

I suffered every last one of the shameful feelings common among abuse victims: *I am to blame, I'm the guilty one, it's my fault, I'm worthless, I'm a loser...* I was angry, I was sad, I was confused. I was disgusted with Jay, disgusted with myself and disgusted with life. It's a lot for a young kid to carry around and I carried this torment for years. It only got worse as I gradually began to make sense of what really went on. *Demons?* Bull! *Brotherly affection?* Hogwash! *Physical illnesses?* An act! Boy was I stupid. The more things began to add up the angrier I became. Like I mentioned, talking to someone surely would have helped but I never went that route. I was too ashamed of myself. It was bad enough that I felt like an idiot; I wasn't about to reinforce someone else's poor opinion of me. My lips remained sealed.

There was one more consequence to my decision to shake Jay off. Though I am not a prophet I saw it coming a mile away. I was forbidden from any future interaction with Roxanne; no visits, no calls, no nothing. It was Jay's order but his mom stood forcefully behind it. I openly confess that I did not honor this ruling completely. Every so often we would sneak calls to each other. On rare occasions I would surprise her at school when class let out. But our contact remained extremely limited during this time. It had to be if I were to avoid a confrontation with Jay. I don't know which was greater, my fear of him or my hatred. I only knew I could never face him again under any circumstances.

*   *   *   *   *

This has been a very difficult chapter to write and it wasn't accomplished without the shedding of tears. However, I'd like to end on a positive note for those who may have suffered abuse, whether it was of a physical, emotional or of a sexual nature.

Precious one, you are not to blame. The one who violated you is the guilty party. Maybe it was someone you looked up to and thought could be trusted. I know how you feel. Listen, it's not your fault. You were set up to be taken advantage of. Don't kick yourself because you didn't see it coming. Your only crime is being a trusting person and that isn't anything to be ashamed of. The real culprit is the one who abused that trust so he could in turn abuse you. And what happened to you does not make you worthless, not in the least. God loves you dearly and places tremendous value upon you. Believe me when I say I understand your pain. Believe also when I tell you that you can find healing. You don't have to be that victim for the rest of your life. In Christ Jesus you can be a 'victor'. We are not there yet but that is exactly where this book leads us. It is the story of a victim who found victory from above. Stay on the journey with me. Please. I truly believe it will be helpful.

Chapter 13

BITTERNESS IS A KILLER
Lessons from Chapter 12

I suppose the right thing to do would have been to forgive Jay. But the right thing always seems to be the hardest thing so I chose to be bitter. Not only was I angry at him I resented my father for what had happened. Honestly, I already despised Dad for checking out on me and my family but the thing with Jay added more fuel to the fire. I felt that if my pop were still around nothing like this would have ever happened. I guess to some degree this is true. It is usually boys without dads that fall prey to such abuses. Such kids tend to have real anger issues as well. I know.

If you ask me, forgiveness is the hardest command in the Bible, period. I have no quarrels with, 'Thou shall not kill.' It's a reasonable thing to ask. I won't argue with laws that prohibit stealing or adultery either. These ideas seem very practical. It's surprising to me that 'Thou shall not bear false witness' would make the top ten but I'm willing to cooperate nevertheless. But forgiveness? Okay, I'll give folks a pass when they make fun of my bald head. And I'll get over it should someone ding the door of my Ford Explorer. But there has to be a line drawn somewhere. As for me, I drew that line with child abuse. This would have made my top ten had I etched some rules in blocks of granite.

There is a problem with drawing lines however, and I feel it is my duty to tell you that whatever you are unwilling to let go of you must carry. The burden is all yours and it gets extremely heavy at times. I should also caution you that these burdens tend to be jam packed with bitterness, and bitterness is a monster which will manifest itself in all kinds of ugly ways. It will affect your relationship with God and with other decent people in your life. They may not want to hang with you much anymore as bitter people aren't known to be fun company. They tend to be very unpleasant and difficult. The only out God offers from bitterness is forgiveness. Trust me on this one, it is the only true out we have.

Jesus taught that we should make things right with our brother before bringing our gifts to the altar.[3] I am of the conviction that this is because bitter hearts are a rip-off to God. We shortchange Him in our worship experience and cheapen His sacrifice to us. A heart full of grace is one that has a generous amount to pour out. If your heart is full of bitterness you haven't much to give, not anything God would want anyway. It's not that He is impressed with the size of our offerings but the purity of them is of great concern to Him. He doesn't want us to get shortchanged either. He wants us to enjoy the ultimate worship experience and bitterness clearly gets in the way of that.

I base my thinking on many passages throughout the Bible but what immediately comes to mind is the sad story of Cain and Abel. This is the first account we have in scripture of gifts being brought to the altar. Cain held back, Abel did not. Cain had issues with his brother, Abel did not. Abel's offering was respected, Cain's was not. Cain grew angry, Abel did not. There is an undeniable pattern here which must not be ignored. After his little charade at the altar Cain's countenance dropped like an anchor into a dry creek bed. He turned into a complete sourpuss. The Lord told him the fix; if he moved in a righteous direction his offerings would be accepted. If not, sin would come a knockin'. But Cain paid no attention to God's counsel

---

[3] Matthew 5:23-24

and allowed his bitterness to fester against his brother. Bitterness killed Cain and Cain killed Abel. End of story.

You may also want to consider the tragic tale of Job. This righteous man had fallen victim to a long series of unfortunate events, plus he was surrounded by a circle some real irritating "friends". With each chapter things just grow bleaker and bleaker. You really start to feel bad for the sorry sap and wonder why God doesn't step in at some point and bail poor Job out. He had to fight bitterness as if he were battling the final stages of cancer. Yet Job becomes a shining example of one who warred against bitterness and won. He doesn't win until the very end of the last chapter, chapter 42. How does he get the victory? He prays for those misguided chums who made his life miserable. Then the Lord blessed Job more than he'd ever been blessed before. And he lived happily ever after.

Bible expositor John Courson refers to forgiveness as a safeguard for our mental heath and emotional stability.[4] This is true. As a pastor I have seen bitterness destroy too many lives. There are those I have pleaded with, almost to the point of tears, to be reconciled with family members or loved ones they were hurt by. Yet they chose to hold onto the offense. Sadly they grow more miserable by the day; they are snappy, irritable and harsh toward others. These are the ones that are always complaining, griping and pouting because they have no friends. Furthermore, it is a wonder to them that God does not hear their prayers. The fact is unforgiveness does hinder our prayers. Jesus gave us a model for prayer which includes the line, *"Forgive us as we forgive others."*[5] This wasn't just randomly thrown in there for purposes of sentimental rhetoric. It was

---

[4] Jon Courson's Application Commentary; page 1253, Ephesians 4:32
[5] Matthew 6:12

included as a condition for our own forgiveness. It is there for us to check our own hearts, and to free us of the baggage that comes with bitterness. It is there to remind imperfect people that anything we might have on our brother, God has a whole lot more on us. After teaching the disciples to pray Jesus immediately elaborated on the issue of forgiveness saying, *"If you forgive the failures of others, your heavenly Father will also forgive you. But if you don't forgive others, your Father will not forgive your failures."* (See Matthew 6:14-15). This divinely inspired footnote to the Lord's Prayer should tell us that forgiveness is serious business and vital to our spiritual well being.

Our expectations are completely out of whack if we think God should forget our numerous offenses when we're not willing to extend lesser grace to others. Jesus makes this clear in the parable of the unfaithful servant.[6] You remember this heartless schlep don't you? He was ready to pound his debtors face in because the guy owed him some chump change. This came immediately after he was forgiven an enormous debt that would have taken more than a lifetime to pay off. Jesus explains at the end of this parable that it is the unforgiving one that really pays in the end. I know this first hand. I paid handsomely when I allowed bitterness to rule my heart. I held onto the offenses of others for seven miserable years. It ate me alive. Things didn't change until I was twenty-two, when I gave my heart [back] to Christ. And I have lived happily ever after.

---

[6] Matthew 18:21-35

Chapter 14

FISTS TO CUFFS

Roxanne was not in the dark with regard to Jay's perverse behavior; she had witnessed enough to know better. To add to Roxanne's horror, painful memories of her own tragic childhood began to surface. Acts of impropriety committed against her by big brother Jay weren't as innocent as she had once perceived. We soon found ourselves in the same capsized boat drifting in a sea of misery, desperation and pain. I was captain and she was first mate and together we shared a common tragedy; we were caught in the same nasty storm and were wounded by a mutual foe. Because I had Roxanne's allegiance and Jay did not, he grew increasingly brutal with her. Young Roxanne was soon deemed the source of all conflict in her home and because of this Mrs. Gowers sorely resented her.

There is no doubt that Roxanne contributed to a lot of yelling, screaming and cursing in her household. She saw it as her only recourse to getting punched and pushed around. This became Jay's only form of contact with his little sister. After I blew him off in the park he stopped talking to her almost completely. He'd only say things like, "Get out of my face!" should he pass her in the hall. Or maybe Roxanne might get a "You bitch!" out of him. These comments were generally followed by a shove or a strike. One time she called me crying because the big ogre had given her a black eye. I felt so bad for Roxanne; she was like a pheasant in the fist of a bear. She was just a tiny little thing, defenseless, barely five-feet-two, just a hundred pounds or so. Jay, on the other hand, stood six-four with over two hundred thirty pounds of raging flesh draped upon a frame of violence.

As big and bad as his brothers were they didn't dare mess with the brute. I had no solutions for Roxanne and I wasn't much of a praying man anymore.

Things grew progressively more explosive between Jay and Roxanne. And Mrs. Gowers wasn't going to sacrifice those golden purse strings Jay held onto by protecting her troubled little girl. So the abuse continued. It continued until Roxanne could take no more. Jay had struck her across the face for the last time and she bailed. She called me from a pay phone in absolute hysterics. "I can't go back home," Roxanne cried. "I'm tired of Jay hitting me." Though I was forbidden from seeing Roxanne I raced to her rescue.

I really didn't know what to do or where to take her. The whole thing was surreal as if I were dreaming or tripping on some PCP slipped into my root beer. My initial instinct was to take Roxanne to the Baptist Church but my trust level was far too low after having been burned there. It is a sad thing when you can't go to a church for help because you fear it would make things worse. Past experience and unhealed wounds had proven that First Baptist would not offer a safe haven for either of us. Then I thought about the FAM house across the street. Tom Fifer was in the business of helping young people, surely he'd know what to do. Roxanne agreed. Before long two desperate souls stood upon an old wooden doorstep waiting to meet with that long haired, bike riding, jean clad, Reverend Tom.

Tom said very little when he showed us in. "You wait here." I was instructed. Then the rev took Roxanne to his back office while I waited in the large living room area. My hopes were high... but not for very long. Before I could sink into the old tattered couch and kick my feet up on the coffee table I heard earsplitting screams escaping from Tom's office. *"WHAT*

ARE YOU DOING TO ME?" Roxanne yelled. *"LET ME GO!!! LET ME GO, DAMMIT!!!"* I went for the office door but it was locked. Blood curdling shrieks continued to echo from behind the hollow walls. *'What is going on?'* I wanted to know. There is no way to describe the horror and helplessness I felt. My entire body was shaking while chills raced frantically up my spine. It was as if I had somehow landed on the set of a Stephen King movie. I didn't know if Roxanne was getting slapped around or raped or what. Maybe Tom was exorcising demons I was just too stupid to recognize. The poor girl was wailing in distress and I was in a state of utter confusion, unable to rescue her.

Suddenly big bad Jay appeared on the scene with Mrs. Gowers. We exchanged no pleasantries; they only greeted me with fierce looking scowls. I just sat there speechless, still trying to figure out what was happening. Tom's office door opened shortly after the villains arrived and there was Roxanne handcuffed to the reverends desk. She was crying and convulsing, her face and blouse were soaked with tears. Evidently the good rev had called Jay to get his side of the story and, whatever it was, the sucker bought it hook, line and sinker. That's when he threw the cuffs on.

Roxanne was quickly released into her molester brother's custody then escorted back by him to her not so happy home. As I watched my sobbing girlfriend disappear Tom began to scold me. "Roxanne's in trouble," he snapped with fire in his eye, "because the two of you have been sneaking off together." The guy didn't know what he was talking about. *'Gee, you're right rev.'* I'm thinking to myself. *'What was I thinking? I'm the bad guy! It certainly couldn't be the jerk who sexually violated his own sister and is now beating on her! My bad, Tom. Can you ever forgive me?'* I didn't respond to the quack. I may have

71

been naïve but I wasn't stupid. A preacher who handcuffs innocent, young gals to his desk wasn't going to be of any help to anyone. How he handled the ordeal with Roxanne was all wrong. It was horrible... *inexcusable!* The only thing Fifer accomplished was - he gave a green light for more abuse to continue. He also affirmed my decision to have nothing more to do with the church. That's about all that came from his reckless response to our cry for help.

Poor Roxanne was left stuck in a terrible bind. Her mom refused to help. The church just made things worse; and regretfully I was in no position to help with Roxanne's dilemma. She had no other choice but to live with a monster and a mad woman. The tension grew worse. It got so bad that Mrs. Gowers considered it a relief when Roxanne wasn't around. Eventually she even allowed her to take off and spend time with me. It was like I was doing Mrs. Gowers a big favor by getting Roxanne out of her frazzled hair. Everyone benefited, until I had to bring her back. Then Jay's ugly fangs would come out again.

* * * * *

For purposes of authenticity I have endeavored to recapture those emotions I felt at the time these events actually occurred. Obviously, mistakes were made at the Baptist Church among a few leaders but this is no attempt to bash them or anyone. These things happened decades ago and Jesus has taught me to forgive. I would also like to reiterate that The First Baptist Church of Van Nuys played a key role in my early Christian walk. The list of those who helped me is long and I'm keeping it. The short list of those who hurt me is left here. My unfortunate experience with First Baptist is merely a hiccup in an otherwise wonderful legacy of faithful service.

As a pastor I encounter many who claim to have been hurt or burned by one church or another. Some have forsaken fellowship altogether because of what happened to them. If that is you, I've been in your shoes. I encourage you not to allow bitterness to isolate you from the family of God. It was grace that brought you into the fold, don't let a lack of grace on your part keep you out. Maybe your expectations of the church were unfair and you need to go back to that flock you walked away from. Or maybe the expectations placed on you by the church were unfair and its good you checked out. But you need to move on. It's time to seek out a fellowship where you can love and be loved. Do not forsake the assembling of the saints.[7]

---

[7] Hebrews 10:25

Chapter 15

ODE TO THE '58 CHEVY

I purchased my first car at sixteen, a 58 Chevy Biscayne. It was an ugly beast with two tones of blue, rusted chrome trim and an oxidized white roof. The paint was bleached out like an ancient barnacle and the body had more dings than a school bell. The matching interior seats were worn out and ripped like a Goodwill sofa set. Though my high mileage vehicle showed a lot of wear and tear, for a fourteen year old jalopy it ran like a Timex watch. I had done okay for $125. Nor could I argue with the payment plan, $25 every other week. That's how often I got paid at Rustler Steakhouse where I bussed tables. It's funny how life goes when you're sixteen. You need a car to get to work and you need to work to get a car. It seems all my money went into my Chevy with insurance, gas and maintenance. My car and my job depended on each other so I kept them both.

It wasn't long after I bought my putter that I received my first traffic violation. This was like a rite of passage for cruising the boulevard. If you didn't have a ticket to wave out your window you weren't anything but a road rookie. I became boulevard worthy on December 31, 1972. It was about eight o'clock in the evening; Roxanne and I were on our way to a New Year's party. I was proceeding to make a lane change on Sherman Way when, all of a sudden, two motorcycle cops decided to pass around my Chevy in pursuit of a speeder. Common sense says that you should never swerve to the left of a vehicle merging in that same direction, even if you have a badge on, but that's exactly what one of the coppers did. The other had a little more sense and passed me to the right. The poor little officer to my left almost took a nasty spill but fortunately for him he quickly regained control of his ride. Nevertheless he wasn't too happy even after saving himself from what may have been a fatal wipeout. The angry policeman hastened ahead to catch up with the speeding vehicle but not before yelling to his partner, *"Get that #*&^* son of a #$^*"* It was obvious from his expletives that he was referring to yours truly.

Before I knew it I was being pulled over for obstructing the way of the foolish. I was confused as to why the citing officer would have me take a sobriety test so early into the evening, besides I was *en route* to a party. It would have made more sense had he caught me on the way home. But he was bent on vengeance and needed a sound reason for pulling me over. So I stood there on one leg, extended both arms, touched the tip of my nose, did the hokey pokey and turned myself around. Following my impeccable performance I was quickly found guilty of sobriety in the first degree. Since there was nothing on the books that would prohibit a person from driving in his right mind I was cited for an unsafe lane change.

I agree that there was an offense committed on that scandalous night, someone had indeed made an unsafe lane change, but it wasn't the squirt in the 58 Chevy. It was that Ponch-wannabe with the trash mouth, the one who referred to me as a *bleepity-bleepity-bleep.* I did not appreciate the vulgar commentary which was expressed by this officer of the law and also felt the citation to be unwarranted. When I told my mother about the incident she recommended that I challenge this charge in court and also share with the judge how I had been assaulted with vile remarks. Either that or I'd pay a handsome fine for something I didn't do. Naturally I decided to have my day in court. However, the citing officer decided not to have a day in court, most likely due to the inevitable embarrassment he would face, so the violation was excused. I was happy the ticket was dismissed but felt robbed of an opportunity to repeat those four-letter words uttered by the foul mouthed cop.

*   *   *   *   *

It is amazing how slow we are to recognize our own sin but when we see that same sin in others we stand ready to condemn. The officer, who obviously exhibited poor driving skills, wanted to condemn me for mine. And then there was me, the biggest trash-mouth of all. I wanted the cop to pay for the very offense I was so often guilty of. Neither of us showed interest in mercy. We were both pointing fingers and both bent on justice. All the while we each had three extra fingers pointing back at ourselves. The fact is, whatever I thought that officer deserved, I deserved ten times more.

Years ago I attended a pastor's conference at Calvary Chapel Vista in California. During the lunch break there was a case of road rage in front of the church. One driver shot the other and the victim died right in the church parking lot. I can't begin to tell you how it changed the mood of our meeting. By God's sovereign design, Pastor Chuck Smith was scheduled to speak next. He had just left the scene of the crime after ministering to the victim's family who were also passengers in the car that was shot at. He was obviously shaken over the ordeal but one thing he said about this incident has never left me. He explained how the police arrived to find fault. They came to identify the guilty party and make an arrest. That's their job. But the paramedics had a different agenda. They weren't concerned with who was guilty or who was innocent. They were simply there to offer help and bring healing. Then Chuck asked us, "Are you a policeman or a paramedic?" I have come to the conclusion, after years of being on patrol, that I'm not called to be a cop. It's not my place to find fault. My job is to bring healing. That's how I roll today.

*   *   *   *   *

My brother, Rick, was a hardcore auto enthusiast. Somehow he had developed an unexplainable affection for my Chevy. I would have preferred his mint condition 67 GTO but Rick enjoyed variety. He could not be satisfied with just one vehicle and would bring home cars like little boys drag home stray puppies. My Chevy definitely had the personality of an abandoned pet and showed great potential for anyone willing to offer it some TLC. Rick was just that kind of guy. Human compassion was something he rarely exhibited but he had a true love for auto repair and restoration.

One afternoon I proceeded to walk out to my car but it was not in the driveway where I had last parked it. I had a sneaking suspicion Rick had 'borrowed' it just like Jimmy and I had borrowed the Datsun from Magic Muffler. My theory proved correct when he pulled up in my long-lost Chevy about an hour later. He was still in the driver's seat when I ran out to confront him. Rick immediately copped an attitude so I decked him. That's right; I hit him square in the kisser. In that very instant after the punch landed upon his sinister smile I thought to myself, *"Self, what did you just do?"* It was the first time I had ever socked my brother and it would prove to be the last. Rick did not take time to consider why I may have been so upset. He simply swung back with a blow so forceful it knocked out one of my teeth. In all fairness, he was not the first to knock out that little chopper. It was actually a cap and had been knocked out with two other teeth years before when I bit asphalt while playing in the street. Nevertheless, Rick had successfully cracked the root in which this cap had been mounted so the whole thing had to be extracted. I wound up with a new tooth on a temporary retainer which actually outlasted its temporary status.

I knew it was time to upgrade vehicles when the axle broke on my Chevy, so I purchased the 63 Mercury Meteor. It had more bells and whistles than the Datsun Jimmy and I stole, *uh, I mean borrowed*; power windows, power locks and an AC that actually blew cool air. It wasn't a GTO but the price was too low to refuse. After I purchased the Meteor, Rick made further desperate pleas for my Chevy. I was understandably not eager to accommodate my brother. I was more interested in making a little cash off my pre-owned vehicle but Rick was relentless and grew increasingly persistent with his appeals. "Please, Terry," he continued to beg. "Let me have your Chevy?" I don't know why I finally gave into him. Perhaps it was because I hoped to win his favor somehow. Maybe it was because Christmastime was upon us and I was feeling especially charitable. Whatever the case I finally surrendered the keys.

A couple of days later, on Christmas Eve, I learned that Rick had turned around and sold my Chevy to the neighbor across the street. We were enjoying holiday cheer when I found out and I got hopping mad for reasons I'm sure you understand. The whole family was together and Mom's boyfriend, Ed, was present for the festivities. Things were not so festive between Rick and me. We glared at each other over glasses of virgin eggnog while bitter fumes seeped through mouths stuffed with butterball cookies. I began to express, perhaps in terms too unkind, my dissatisfaction with Rick's despicable self-serving behavior. Then Ed made a snide comment I didn't appreciate. My frustration suddenly shifted from Rick to Ed. I picked that moment to finally repeat all those terrible things spoken by the foul-mouthed cop. My mother had never been more humiliated in her life. At least that is what she claimed and I had no cause to doubt her.

*   *   *   *   *

79

The third chapter of James' epistle has much to say about the tongue. In James 3:4 the tongue is compared to a small rudder of a huge ship. I might liken it to the steering wheel of a 58 Chevy. The idea here is that wherever we maneuver that tiny flapper the rest of our flesh is sure to follow. James goes on to describe the uncontrolled tongue as a small flame ignited by hell which can quickly set off a huge blaze.[8] No doubt the foul mouthed policeman had set a fire under me. And my mother was quite inflamed when I cussed out her beau. The most alarming thing James says about that puny little muscle mass is, "No man can tame the tongue!"[9] Take it from someone who has tried, the apostle is right. We've got to hand that little rudder over to God. Only He can control it. And He'll never steer you wrong!

---

[8] James 3:5-6
[9] James 3:7-8

Chapter 16

THE ODD COUPLE
Flaming Red Hair

Van Nuys High School has achieved some claim to fame with an impressive cast of famous alumni. Marilyn Monroe went there. So did Robert Redford and Natalie Wood. If I had flunked out a few times I could have graduated with Paula Abdul. You may have had a virtual tour of Van Nuys High without even realizing it. *Fast Times at Ridgemont High* was filmed there. So was *Rock and Roll High School*. Jimmy's brother Vincent starred in that film with the Ramones. However, the seventies left our school in limbo. The Van Nuys High Wolves, with a woeful series of consecutive losses, had earned a reputation as the worst football team in the entire valley. Our cheerleading squad was a total embarrassment. We really could have used some of Paula Abdul's slick choreography during this time. While San Fernando High was doing cheers to cutting edge scores like *Shaft* we were shouting off to the theme to the *Mickey Mouse Club* show. Don't laugh, I'm totally serious. But the 70's did produce a glimmer of hope for Van Nuys High, one that should have altered the entertainment industry forever... the comedic writing duo of Van Patten and Michaels.

*   *   *   *   *

It was probably Jimmy who spurred my short-lived interest in small screenwriting. When they offered 'Writing for TV' as an elective at Van Nuys High, Jimmy and I agreed to take it together. This was only fair. I had conned him into taking ceramics class with me. (And might I say he didn't take very well to the mud.)

Mr. Foster, a short, stout and jolly fellow, taught Writing for TV. He wore horn-rimmed glasses like Drew Carrey, and he looked, laughed and acted like him too. Mr. Foster was one of the few teachers at Van Nuys High that I actually liked. I think he was also one of the few instructors that didn't hate my guts, so we were pretty compatible as far as student-teacher relationships go. Foster was also the kind of guy you could poke fun at and get a hearty chuckle out of. Ridicule was not only sanctioned in his classroom it was highly encouraged. And it was no secret that Mr. Foster was fond of the suds. He would share about the crazy escapades he and his beer drinking buddies enjoyed in the beer bars they frequented. To make him feel at home students would get to class before he arrived and write 'BEER' on the chalk board in bold, dusty letters. He'd sheepishly smile like Drew Carrey and laugh it off.

Foster spent the first couple weeks explaining the basics of small screen writing. "You need conflict then resolution," he summarized. "Now pair off and write a script." The assignment was to draft a thirty minute episode for a program already airing on television. Jimmy and I instantly pulled our young minds and graffiti laden desk chairs together. I didn't even have to ask him which show he'd like to consider. He had recently appeared on the sitcom 'The Odd Couple' with Jack Klugman and Tony Randall and had become an instant fan of the series. Comedy was also up my alley so we settled on Jimmy's recommendation. I believe we actually made a pretty decent writing team, with his creative ideas and my dry wit.

The conflict was Jimmy's suggestion. Tony Randall's anal retentive character, Felix, would land in jail on a false purse snatching charge. The entire script would focus on his feeble attempts to get bailed out of the slammer. All the while this most unlikely criminal would dig himself a deeper hole by trying to explain the series of dubious events which led to his most unfortunate predicament. The idiotic Officer Murray, a reoccurring character on the Odd Couple series, would play a key role in this particular episode.

Jimmy and I would discuss our ideas quite audibly and whenever Murray's name was mentioned a freckly redheaded kid on the other side of the classroom would think we were addressing him. His name was also Murray. He was kind of a geeky dude with a huge wad of hair shaped like a pregnant tumbleweed. I must confess that Jimmy and I enjoyed picking on this fellow. Every time the name Murray came up in our script writing we would say it loud and proud, and usually in the form of a question, *"... and then MURRAY?"* Without fail our red headed friend would respond, *"What?"* So we would egg him on...

"Okay, so they lock Felix up in this slimy cell," Jimmy would say.
"Yeah!" I would add, "And he's polishing the bars with his handkerchief."
"And there's a drunk passed out behind him..."
"And a mean looking thug backs away from Felix because he thinks he's nuts..."
"Good, good..." Jimmy beams, "Then *MURRAY?*"
[*"What?"* our freckly classmate responds.]
"Then *MURRAY?* says..." Jimmy continues with a laugh, "Felix, why are you here?"
"For stealing."
"And *MURRAY?* replies, 'Oh, Felix, I never thought you'd do such a thing.'"
"No, you don't understand *MURRAY?* I was just going to the store to get some furniture polish."
"And *MURRAY?* says, 'Oh, Felix, did you have to steal it? I

would have bought some for you.'"

"*MURRAY?* I'm not accused of stealing furniture polish,' Felix explains. 'It was a purse!'"

"And *MURRAY?* shakes his head in disbelief. 'Shame on you Felix!'"
"No *MURRAY?* It wasn't me!"

All the while Jimmy and I are blurting out Murray's name the word *"What?" is* ricocheting across the room. This went on for days and before long others in the class were chiming in. *"MURRAY?"* Greg would say. *"What?"* he would answer. Moments later Sam would belt out, *"MURRAY?"* and he would respond, *"What?"* Everyday the poor kid's name would bounce off the walls and the entire class would laugh at you know *"What?"* Though he was a good sport about it, Murray wore a huge target on his back daily. I imagine other kids in school picked on him as well. He just had that look which said, "I'm a big weenie so lemme' have it!" Honestly, I started to feel bad for the guy. Getting picked on wasn't foreign territory for me either; I knew how it felt. But I never thought things would escalate so far. What began as innocent teasing turned into Murray becoming an object of continual ridicule.

I think Greg Headley was the hardest on Murray, he sat right behind him. Greg would lean close to the back of his bushy head and yell, *"MURRAY?"* so loud he'd jump out of his seat. It was also Greg who set Murray's hair ablaze. He didn't mean to, it just started out as a gag. Greg pulled a lighter out of his pocket, lit it, and then held it near Murray's huge mass of red frizz. It was just for laughs but then the small flickering flame got a tad too close. Within an instant, *poof,* Murray's hair was on fire. Greg responded quickly by whacking his inflamed neighbor over the head with his notebook. Murray didn't even know his hair was burning and couldn't understand why Greg was beating him so fiercely. It all happened so fast. Thankfully no one was seriously injured but the classroom was left with the pungent odor of smoldering locks. To this day I am uncertain as to whether Murray ever found out it was the smell of his own.

After Murray's bad hair day Jimmy and I lightened up on the poor guy to concentrate on our assignment. Weeks later we finally finished our draft. Mr. Foster must have had a few *drafts* when he read it as he gave our work a pretty high score. I got to hang onto the script for a couple weeks so my Mom could read it, after that I never saw it again. Jimmy was convinced it was worthy of production and hoped his dad could pass it on to the producers of *The Odd Couple*. I was in favor of this idea but, unfortunately, the creators of the show were not.

Taking 'Writing for TV' remains one of my fondest memories of high school. Jimmy and I had a blast collaborating together and Mr. Foster was a real kick. I only wish we would have treated Murray differently. It seems that Jimmy and I instigated an avalanche of ill treatment upon an otherwise good-natured kid. I suppose this is just another fine example of how that little tongue can spark a nasty fire.

Chapter 17

THE COST OF A FIREBIRD
Only Fools Rush Sin

By the time I was seventeen I had already gone through several cars. They were all cheap heaps I had paid very little for. But I was in a brand new league with my 67 Firebird. Sorry was the day when I sold her to buy a Pinto. That catchy jingle, *'Ford Has a Better Idea'* was not a tribute to that lemon. My 'Bird, however, now that was a peach. And mine was a clean machine, no dents, dings or scratches like the other pre-owned-times-twenty junkers I had driven. The 'Bird was midnight blue with a black interior and tinted windows. She wasn't really built for speed, just a six cylinder with three in the tree, but she was pretty. This was no low dollar vehicle either. I paid for it in blood. The honest to goodness truth is I had to suffer a serious butt kickin' to get her. Had that not happened there never would have been a lawsuit... Had there never been a lawsuit I never would have been sitting pretty in a cherried-out Firebird at seventeen.

*   *   *   *   *

I was still a runt when the incident happened, a fifteen year old punk. Little Rick (not to be confused with my brother Big Rick) was only thirteen. We were neighbors. He lived in the foster home about six or seven doors down from my house. Little Rick was a studious fellow. Unlike me he took school seriously. His dream was to be a doctor like his dad, the dad he never really got to know. I suppose that's what we had in common, other than that there wasn't much else. He was Jewish, I wasn't. He was academic, not this guy. He had common sense; I didn't have a lick of it. But we each had a mutual emptiness we could share in and that seemed to be enough.

Little Rick and I hadn't ventured too far from our street; we were just a few blocks away in the industrial area. We always met interesting people and found peculiar stuff when we combed the alleys. It was a scavenger's paradise, a galleria of sorts for junk collectors. One could always count on Redkin's Laboratory to throw out a lot of foul smelling hair products. Then there was the place that packaged dehydrated foods like the astronauts eat; their dumpster offered a lovely array of edibles. One time we found an entire load of defective Bennelli Motorcycle gas tanks, they were free for the taking! Pro surfer Ernie Tanaka manufactured surfboards and Grand Prix legend Bruce MacLaren built his race car in the alleys of Van Nuys. This is how we spent our time as kids; if we weren't cruising the boulevard we were roaming the alleys.

We had just come out of an alley onto the sidewalk when calamity came to greet us. Little Rick had already finished his soda and was wearing the empty can under his shoe. I was still sipping on my pop as the delightful sound of tin scraping on cement trailed behind me. It wasn't long before the racket ceased. The abused can clutching to the sole of Rick's sneaker finally broke free. It remained just steps behind him as he proceeded forward. There the lonely and wrinkled container lay in front of Hoffman VW Auto Repair. That's when the angry grease monkey appeared from behind the hood of a Volkswagen Bug. Before we could say, *"Estut mir leid!"* he came out screaming like a banshee. In a loud German accent the mechanic tore into Little Rick with words I shant repeat. I will only say that I did not like the tone he took with my little friend. Something had to be done.

I quickly guzzled down the rest of my soda, yelled a few choice words back at the creep then tossed my empty tin can onto his immaculately clean lot. This did not please the temperamental auto technician; he came tearing after us like a rabid pit bull. My advice to Little Rick was the same given to me by Jimmy when we crashed the Datsun, *"Run!"* He heeded my counsel without hesitation and we took off toward our street with a madman hot on our tails. Once we lost Mr. Goodwrench we hid behind a large bush, hyperventilating like two scared rabbits. "If he sees us you run home," I instructed Rick between heavy gasps for breath, "I'll head for the alley." We both knew who this maniac would come running after once we separated. Being the more mature one the martyr would have to be me. Perhaps it was a rare moment of nobility on my part or maybe I was just used to getting my butt kicked. Whatever the case, this was how it had to go down. Little Rick would not suffer the consequences of my dastardly deed.

Within seconds we were spotted and our plan was executed immediately. As predicted the chase continued without Little Rick. My heart was pounding with fear as I poured every ounce of energy I had into my flight. I bolted for the alley with my pursuer tailing close behind. Weaving back and forth between parked vehicles I stayed ahead of him by several paces. But then... a car came driving toward me from the opposite end of the alley. It was another mechanic from the garage. I was rapidly being boxed in from both sides with nowhere to run. Finally I stopped in my tracks, threw up my scrawny little arms and cried, "I surrender!" I've seen this work on spaghetti westerns but it didn't change my luck any. The crazed mechanic continued to charge at me full speed ahead then, *KAPOW!* With the force of his entire bodyweight behind him he landed a punch to my face which sent me sailing. I crashed to the ground with a painful thud. He then picked me up by the scruff of the neck and slammed my forehead into the hard asphalt. That's when I saw pretty stars swirling in my head, the ones Wiley Coyote sees when he takes a terrible spill. Once I came to, my assailant dragged me by the shirt back to Hoffman VW Auto Repair to pick up the soda can I threw.

By the time I returned home I was a bloody mess. My mom freaked when she saw me and wanted fast answers so I recounted the whole tragic story. It is true that certain words were omitted when quoting myself but I did not want to shock my mother as when I had cussed out her beau. That notwithstanding, Mom didn't hesitate to call the police. They came, took a statement and shot some lovely pictures of my battered face and the big greasy handprint on the back of my new denim shirt which, by the way, was quite torn up after the scuffle. My pictorial would appear in a civil court hearing a couple years later and help me in my plight for procuring more reliable transportation.

It turned out that the two mechanics responsible for my misfortune were both brothers and business partners by the name of Hoffman. They weren't as big as I remembered when we met up again at the courthouse. In the two years it took for my civil case to be heard by an L.A. County judge I had gone through a drastic growth spurt. Actually I stretched like a rubber band to nearly six feet tall but my weight remained around one-hundred and thirty pounds. Nevertheless, I was now taller than the Hoffman brothers and Mom was concerned that I might not be able to convince a judge that the one brother had kicked the crud out of me. Their defense was that I tripped and fell but, thankfully, the judge didn't buy it. When the settlement finally came I went car shopping and I owe it all to the Hoffman's for giving me the 'Bird. *And a bird in the garage is better than two dodos in the bush!*

*   *   *   *   *

I was playing around with my Bible software program recently and was amazed to discover that the word 'fool' is used thirty-nine times in the book of Proverbs. This prompted me to do a little further investigation so I searched the term 'foolish' which is used eleven times. Then I looked up 'foolishness' and found nine uses of that expression. Rounding the list was 'folly' which has thirteen occurrences in Solomon's book of wisdom. If you do the math with me you'll discover that variations of the word 'fool' are used a total of seventy-two times in Proverbs, a book which is only thirty-two chapters long. Many of these proverbs connect foolishness with a loose tongue, which was certainly true in my case.

Proverbs goes on record to state that many of man's troubles can be avoided through sound wisdom. The other side of that is we can expect misfortune when we choose the way of a fool. I'm not suggesting that I deserved getting my rear whipped by Mr. Goodwrench but the truth is I certainly could have avoided it. This was a pattern in my life; my mouth got me into a heap of trouble over and over again. Just as the Proverbs say, *"As a dog returns to his vomit, so a fool repeats to his own folly."* (See Proverbs 26:11) Solomon also wrote that it is better to meet a bear robbed of her cubs than to cross the path of a fool.[10] Now; you'd have to be a pretty big fool to go up against a mother grizzly wouldn't you? The problem with fools is they go up against each other which can be even scarier. At least mama bear is in a protective mode but fools are just plain reckless. Mr. Hoffman and I were worse than two grizzlies going at it. And both of us brought calamity upon ourselves which potentially

---

[10] Proverbs 17:12

could have harmed others, like Little Rick for example.

The good news is that no one has to be a fool. Please do not think that some are destined to be that way while others are naturally wise. As a matter of fact, folly is what comes most natural to people while wisdom cries out in the streets, "Take me, I'm yours!" If you don't believe me just read the first chapter of Proverbs.[11] James also tells us that God is quite generous with wisdom and will give it to anyone who asks for it.[12] Sadly, wisdom has very few takers. My hope is that you'll take God up on his generous offer if you haven't already. Wisdom begins when we respectfully look up to Him.[13]

---

[11] Proverbs 1:20-23
[12] James 1:5
[13] Proverbs 9:10

Chapter 18

MY NAME IS NACHO

After graduating high school in 1974 my immediate plan was to leave home and get my own place. It was something I truly felt to be in everybody's best interest: Mom would have one less mouth to feed, I'd escape the oppression of my older brother and, if things worked out, I could get Roxanne out of an abusive situation. My boss, Tony, was sympathetic to my plight and offered me a full time cooking position at Rustler Steakhouse. Tony also owned an apartment complex in North Hollywood. He said he'd knock off half the rent if I wanted to live there. In exchange I could help manage the complex by collecting rent money from tenants and keeping the property tidy. I found his proposition appealing and quickly signed off on the deal before even seeing what I was getting into. That was my first mistake.

Roxanne was also very excited about the prospect of moving out. Her home situation had not improved and she was basically unwanted there. We had one little snag to work out though; Roxanne was only fifteen years old. Knowing how Mrs. Gowers felt about her I was pretty confident she'd cut her loose. As a matter of fact, parental consent wasn't an issue at all; it was a piece of cake. I simply knocked on Mrs. Gowers door and asked if Roxanne could live with me. She was totally on board with the idea. Her one and only worry was saving face with the welfare department so we agreed, *for the record*, Roxanne still lived at home should anyone ask. Other than that Mrs. Gowers was quite happy with the arrangement; for her it meant one less headache.

When I announced to my mom that I would be getting an apartment she wasn't jet hot on the idea. The truth is she tried like the dickens to talk me out of it. At the same time, she was going to charge me rent unless I checked into community college or a trade school. Furthering my education didn't seem like a bad idea at all. I really wanted to yet I felt other obligations were more pressing at the time. I was on an urgent mission, a rescue mission. Any ambitions of my own would have to be put on hold. Besides, if I was going to pay rent I'd rather exercise my squatter's rights elsewhere. The decision was final. But to soften the blow I did not tell Mom about my arrangement with Roxanne. She already had strong objections to our relationship and this would surely have put her over the edge.

Neither Roxanne nor I ever saw the apartment complex until the day we moved in. Like I said, this was a gross mistake. The place was an absolute slum. It looked as if every gang in the San Fernando Valley had tagged it with graffiti. Walls were bashed in, windows were covered with foil and the courtyard was littered with mounds of trash. It was not a welcoming sight even for someone with standards as low as mine were at the time. Roxanne and I held our noses as we moved our garage sale goods into our unit, which wasn't any more inviting on the inside than it was on the outside. But at least our apartment was conveniently located in the barrio so we didn't have to travel too far to catch a good street rumble.

I was not opposed to living in an all Chicano apartment building in the barrio. However, I did fear because of their gang associations that they may object to a *gringo* and a *negrita* in the hood. My concerns were validated on that first day we moved in. Roxanne and I were not offered a very warm reception but only met with sneers and contemptible eyes. Little did they know - there was a new slum-lord in town.

It didn't take long to learn that the thugs didn't ever sleep at our gang infested tenement. They'd stay up late in the grungy courtyard yapping, drinking Coors beer and playing their music for all of North Hollywood to enjoy. And for whatever reason, they avoided toilets like Willie Nelson avoids the IRS, preferring to mark their territory like junkyard dogs. It was also apparent that these gangs were opposed to the idea of trash receptacles. The courtyard served a dual function as a social square and a dumping ground for beer cans or whatever else these hoodlums stuck in their faces. This did not make my job easy. After all, I was the one who had to pick up after these guys! It was a task which proved to be impossible.

Each day I would pick up every stinkin' beer can but within about a twelve hour period they'd mysteriously reappear. After a few weeks of this I had had about all I could take. I wasn't going to be some little white fairy with a feather duster cleaning up after gang-bangers. That's when I decided some policy was in order. So I printed up a couple of rules, very simple rules: no more drinking in the courtyard and curfew would be at ten o'clock. That was it, two clear-cut policies which I courageously posted in **BIG BOLD** letters in the courtyard. Gang-bangers don't take to policy very well. The very next day the quad was filled with empty cans and the rules which I so valiantly posted were crumpled up and left upon my doorstep. But none of this deterred me from posting them again.

Later that evening I heard a knock on my door. When I answered, there was a mountain sized man standing there to greet me. He sported a shaved head and a fu-man-chu mustache. He had giant muscles rippling out of his white wife-beater tank top. He did not yell or growl or swear. Actually, he spoke in a very subdued tone. "Hello, my name is Nacho," our visitor calmly announced, "And here are your rules." Mr. Nacho handed me a wadded up piece of paper then explained to me the demographics of our community. "There are many of us," he warned, "And only one of you." By 'one of you' I was pretty certain he wasn't referring to Rustler Steakhouse employees. Nacho ended our little chat by telling me it would be best if Roxanne and I found another place to dwell. I thanked the dear man and told Roxanne to start packing.

I suppose we could have stood our ground and defended our right to remain there. But, honestly, the North Hollywood apartments weren't suitable for sewer rats to live in and they certainly weren't worth fighting over. The gang-bangers were welcome to keep it for themselves as far as I was concerned. So Roxanne and I heeded the sound counsel of our distinguished neighbor with the bulging biceps and got the heck outta' there as quick as a flea hop.

It didn't take long for us to find another apartment. From North Hollywood we moved back to Van Nuys, just a few short blocks away from Rustler Steakhouse and not too far from Van Nuys High where Roxanne was still attending school. She completed her entire high school education while she lived with me. But living together proved an impossible challenge for both of us. Emotionally, we just weren't ready. We were troubled kids with a lot of baggage and unresolved issues. Because of this we fought often. Things would get very verbal with a lot of yelling and swearing, and often it would escalate to physical altercations. When Roxanne got mad she would tear after me like a Tasmanian devil and I would give her a good smack from time to time. Nacho was not the last person to run us out of an apartment. Because we were so violent and disruptive we received eviction notices from each of the various places we lived in. Looking back, I didn't save Roxanne from anything.

*   *   *   *   *

I have done a lot of thinking about marriage verses the idea of living together with someone. The question is; what makes a couple choose one rather than the other? The conclusion I've come to is that living together offers convenience while marriage requires commitment. I don't think there is any commitment between two people as serious as marriage. Within this divine institution the two have become one. The husband has taken a vow to put his wife's wants, needs and interests above his own and she has promised to do the same for him. And marriage offers no outs. It's 'till death do you part. This is not true of the couple who simply live together. They do score on some of the benefits of marriage but the two are not one. When I was in this kind of arrangement with Roxanne, we were two individuals and each of us put our own interests first. That's probably why we could never get along. The other thing is either of us could walk out the door at anytime which is what eventually happened. That's what makes living together so convenient. You can be selfish and you can leave. In marriage you don't have the liberty to do either.

As I thought about this I began also to ponder how man relates to God. Some interact with Him through religion while others connect more intimately; they have a relationship with the Lord. Interestingly enough, it's the difference between 'living together' and 'marriage'. Religion is man's way of living together _with_ God and it offers the liberty of putting one's own interests ahead of His. Relationship is about living _in_ God with the desire to please Him first. Religion also has a way of creating great distance between man and God. Not so when we are in a relationship with the Lord. The two become one. Never in God's Word do we find Him inviting us to be religious. He does, however, invite us into a relationship. His proposal was made from a cross.

Even now He waits at the altar of every broken heart to hear lovers say, "I do."

"Let us rejoice, be happy, and give him glory because it's time for the marriage of the lamb. His bride has made herself ready. She has been given the privilege of wearing dazzling, pure linen. This fine linen represents the things that God's holy people do that have his approval." Revelation 19:7-8

Chapter 19

A TOOTH FOR A TOOTH

I must tell you about the time Roxanne got her tooth knocked out. You'll probably think very highly of me when I tell you that I personally paid to have it repaired with my own hard earned cash. Save your kudos. That exalted opinion will quickly plummet once you learn I was the one who knocked it out in the first place. It's true, I did. We got into a vicious argument in the car. Things got real ugly and I flew out of control. Then... I back-handed her... right in the kisser. I know exactly what you are thinking, there is no excuse for this kind of brutality, and you are absolutely right. I take no pride in what I did. Somehow timid little Terry morphed into a big pig, a big angry pig. Yes, I had moments when I could be nice but they didn't make up for the times I was mean.

There are folks who say, "If I could do it all over again I wouldn't change anything." Well, I'm not one of those proud people. I wish I could say such a thing but unfortunately I can't. I do have regrets. If I could amend the past I would do it in a heartbeat. There are things I have done that I'd like to take back. Many things! One of them is hitting Roxanne. It ranks up there as one of my most shameful moments in life. I am relieved to know that the Lord isn't holding this against me, or anything else I've done for that matter. But even though my slate is now clean, it gives me a sick feeling to know that I took out the tooth of a sixteen year-old girl. This would be a do-over if I could rewind history. Thankfully, though, I'm not the person I once was. The good Lord put to death that angry beast in me. I only wish that beast would have died sooner... Before I whacked Roxanne!

Sadly, Roxanne's front teeth were quite brittle to begin with. And there were others just like it. Way before I even met her, one of her brothers had been swinging her by the ankles and when he let go she went flying. Her teeth were quite buck so when her face hit the ground - out popped two pair of choppers, roots and all. After removing the nerves the dentist just crammed them back into her face. He had bored out the insides leaving Roxanne's teeth nothing more than dead, hollow shells. I was not the first to knock that sad tooth out, nor was I the last. But I was there to witness the final round.

Some of us at Rustler Steakhouse decided to go on a Saturday afternoon picnic. I don't know who decided on Lanark Park, it was way on the other side of the valley, but that's where the twelve of us ended up. It seemed peaceful enough when we arrived and provided everything you'd hope a city park to offer: big shade trees, acres of lawn, picnic benches and barbeque pits. Oh, and did I mention restrooms? It is important that I do because that is where the conflict began.

It wasn't long after we spread our blankets that a couple gals from our group went to visit the stalls. They returned quite perturbed. Some teenage boys had followed them into the facilities to spy on them. Not only did they watch these young ladies do their business, the little twerps teased them about it. This did not set well with their noble beaus, Kenny and John, who became very upset over the matter. Shortly after the perv report came in we spotted the suspects a short distance away. They were gazing our direction and laughing like court jesters. Like knights in shining armor, Kenny and John rose to defend the honor of their distressed damsels and gallantly charged over to confront the adolescent barbarians. Because of their wee stature the potty dwellers were spared the thrashing they deserved and were each chastised in words uncomplimentary to the King James English. We promptly celebrated the humbling of these foul peasants by devouring fried chicken with bare hands and tossing down tin goblets of foamy ale. But then the delinquents returned.

The kids whistled out to us, challenging our peaceful group to combat. We might have accepted had there not been an army behind them. And had we been aware of their gang affiliation those boys may not have received such a harsh scolding. We were outnumbered by at least five to one, and the cholo gang came armed with bottles, belts and bats. The leader of the pack bore a strong resemblance to Nacho who had chased me out of that delightful community in North Hollywood. Fearing for our safety we attempted to engage in peace

100

talks. Kenny, who earlier enjoyed success as diplomat to the two potty pervs, quickly appointed himself as leader of our gang. Negotiations did not go well between Kenny and Nacho's look-alike. Talking turned to yelling and yelling turned to, well... Kenny just hauled off and popped the guy in the face. The cholo gang did not take a liking to this severe course of action. They quickly marched in and surrounded our tribe of six gals and six guys, strategically positioning themselves for battle in a cause no greater than protecting their right to prowl around public toilets and watch girls pee.

Barbara, who worked with me on dayshift, had brought her mother and stepfather, Ted, to our outing. This middle-aged black fellow had about ten guys on him and they were using his tired body as a punching bag. I felt the need to rescue the poor gentleman. Not being a strong fighter I wasn't sure what to do but I was determined to bail ol' Ted out. Being all mouth and no muscle I used my quick wit to distract the merciless cholos. "Boys and girls," I announced, "I'm sure we can all sit down and discuss this over a cup of coffee." They turned around to see what kind of idiot would say such a screwy thing in the midst of a gang jump. Idiot or not my silly scheme offered at least some benefit. More than half the group pulled away from Ted and he safely escaped the wrath of the dreadful potty punks. The downside to all this was they came after me. One of the gangsters took off his belt and started doing figure eights with the buckle end sailing through the air. That was my cue to run.

We all fled, each pursued by at least four bloodthirsty cholos. These thugs even went after the girls. It puzzled me that they would exhibit such unbecoming hostility toward gals who disagreed with their bathroom antics. But this was their cause and they were bent on defending it, even if it meant that a few ladies got hurt in the process. I eventually caught up with Roxanne who also had a few of these toilet crusaders tailing close behind her. Before long they successfully chased us both down. From that moment on everything happened rather quickly. Police helicopters came and circled the area. The restroom ruffians started running like roaches on a hot griddle. One by one the creeps surrounding Roxanne and I disappeared. But before taking off, one of them threw a punch at Roxanne and knocked out her tooth.

A few of us got banged up pretty bad but I imagine things would have been a whole lot worse had the cops not shown up. When LAPD officers arrived on park grounds to investigate the situation we insisted on pressing charges. But they were less than willing to accommodate us, reasoning that they didn't have adequate resources to round up all the guilty parties. That's when I understood why there was such a gang problem in Los Angeles. Law enforcement pretty much left them alone. That was the 70's though. Hopefully things are different today. If not, praise God I now live in Texas!

*   *   *   *   *

It would be hypocritical of me to condemn the thug who took out Roxanne's tooth. I hadn't been any less of a jerk when I popped her one. I've often wondered how I could have done such a thing. How could I stoop so low? I now know the answer and I don't like it: it's my nature. In spite of all its miserable flaws there was a time I fought hard to keep this unruly side of me. There were other things about it I wasn't so eager to let go of. But it was a package deal, all or nothing. Hanging on to the old nature meant I'd have to get use to blowing my stack and acting stupid. But God offered me an attractive new nature in exchange for the old ugly one. I couldn't see turning Him down, especially in light of the huge price He paid for the upgrade.

People say they can change but I don't believe that for a New York minute. I've never seen a case where anyone has been successful through their own efforts. I've observed some noble attempts but eventually these folks all jump back into the same mire or they find an even worse hole to wallow in. Here are the sad statistics: most all molesters are repeat molesters, most all alcoholics are chronic alcoholics and most all abusers will abuse again. My late father-in-law, who practiced psychiatry his entire life would say, "Tigers don't change their stripes." It's true. Psychiatrists and Bible teachers don't see eye to eye on very much but that is one thing we can agree upon. People can't change, it's that simple. I've tried and, believe me, it just doesn't work. *But God!* Tigers can't change their stripes but God can change them! By the same token, it is impossible for man to change his own nature. But with God all things are possible! He does change lives. He has changed mine and countless others. The Lord doesn't change His own stripes but He stands willing to re-stripe anyone who humbly comes to Him. And we can be thankful He doesn't change His own stripes. It took His to remove ours. By His stripes we are healed![14]

---

[14] Isaiah 53:5

Chapter 20

BON MICHEL

I knew it was more than just a social visit when Dad arranged for me, my brother and two sisters to all have dinner together. This was the first (and last) time the four of us ever sat at the same table with him since the divorce. We met at *Benihana's* on Avenue of the Stars for some fry-it-in-your-face Japanese cuisine. The chef held us spellbound with his nail-biting knife tossing and dare-devilish fire throwing but when the show was over Dad had something important to say. "As you probably know," he lamented. "Your mother is suing me." It wasn't news to us, we were well aware of the fact. "If she wins," he continued, "I will have no other choice but to leave the country."

That was his pitch. I wasn't quite sure how it would affect any of us, though. By this time, it did not seem things could get anymore estranged than they already were. I had even wondered if it would be easier for us if Dad lived somewhere in Timbuktu. At least then we could justify a distant relationship with our father. Nevertheless, he appealed for our allegiance so we wouldn't have to suffer the terrible fate of losing all hope of any future contact. We each sat there with blank looks and piled chopsticks unloading into our hungry faces. In spite of the impressive meal and his tear-jerking plea we could not be swayed. "I'll write to you Dad," I thought to myself as grains of rice tap-danced atop my slippery tongue, "I'll even pay for the postage myself."

Though I agreed with my mother on the issue I didn't want to get dragged into the middle of this whole ugly mess. If Dad didn't pay child support then Mom was entitled to back pay, it was that simple. I didn't see how vouching for Mom or Dad would change anything. What could any of us kids possibly say that would make any difference? The facts spoke for themselves. Either money was owed or it wasn't. That was for a judge to decide not me or Rick or my sisters. And honestly, I begrudged the fact that we grew up poor while Dad's second family lived high on the hog in Newport Beach. I would shed no tears if they were reduced to living on the same side of the tracks as we did. Not only did Dad fail to win my sympathy I resented him for what I felt was an underhanded attempt to pit me against my own mother. I saw her as the victim, not him. Her world had been shattered when she learned of his secret life.

$$* \quad * \quad * \quad * \quad *$$

It was while my dad was 'on assignment' in France 'covering a story' when mom learned of his affair and the love-child it produced. A daycare center contacted our home phone regarding a bounced check. Initially, Mom was certain there was some kind of gross error. "Are you married to Clete Harmon?" the mysterious caller asked. Mom assured her that she was. The questioning continued, "Your name isn't Rosey?" Mom assured her that it wasn't, though she was very familiar with a certain secretary named Rosey. "Tabitha isn't your daughter?" the puzzled voice continued to inquire. This was followed by a resounding, "No!" Dad wasn't covering his tracks very well and by this time Mom was growing increasingly suspicious of his extended stay in France. She would soon discover that his trip was all pleasure and no business, and that he was gallivanting around Paris with his secretary the entire time.

Other curious calls came to the house while Dad was away. People involved in a porno ring were also trying to locate Dad and Rosey. Mom took note of the name of their underground publication, went to wherever they sold this kind of smut in the early sixties, and bought a few issues. I'll never forget when my brother and I stumbled upon these disgusting rags. I was only about eight or nine at the time. It was the holiday season and we were snooping around to see where Mom hid the Christmas presents. Next thing I knew, Rick was calling me to the hall closet. In his hand was a porn magazine with our family cabin cruiser, the *Bon Michel*, pictured smack-dab on the front cover. On our boat was a familiar blonde, buck naked. It was Rosey. There were others on the good ship, both men and women, all totally nude from head to toe. My fondest childhood memories took place on the Bon Michel but now the crude, naked bodies tainted them all. The inside cover of this graphic magazine listed Clete Harmon as chief editor and president.

I can't even begin to describe what it does to a kid when he discovers his dad is involved with a cheap porno publication. The very man who took me to mass every Sunday was pictured in the cabin at the wheel, steering a boat load of nudists to smutzville. To this day I can still see him in his skipper's hat with that familiar smile I'd grown to know so well. On deck, in the buff, was the woman he left my mother for. She was all over this magazine. And all over the boat... *our family boat! The Bon Michel!* My heart sank to my stomach as we flipped through the pages. *'How could they?'* I grieved. It was on this very boat my family spent most of our summer vacations. Together we enjoyed countless trips to Catalina Island. We ate, slept, laughed and played on this boat. The bow was territory marked by my own barf; breakfast, lunch and dinner. Disgusting, maybe. But not as repulsive as what I saw when Rick took me through a pornographic tour of my old playground, the Bon Michel. I was devastated. I did not tell you in the opening chapter but I confronted my dad about this when we had our big blow out. I asked him why he got involved in the pornography business. He told me he did it for my mother. I lost it when I heard his answer. It appalled me that he would try to dignify something so shameful. I wasn't about to let that one go. "You did it for a mother alright, but not mine." He offered no response.

How Dad maintained such a scandalous secret life as a public figure amazes me to this day. He was a local television celebrity of sorts, seen daily on KTLA news. He ran for congress and city council as a conservative candidate. He was consistently in the public eye, hob-knobbed with other well known TV and showbiz icons, and was an active member of St. Cyril's Catholic Church. All the while he was juggling two homes and two families, and publishing pornographic material that would make Hugh Hefner blush.

*　　*　　*　　*　　*

In light of what I knew my conscience would not allow me to vouch for my unfaithful father. Nor could I side against my devoted mother who raised me single-handedly. Mom had suffered enough heartbreak to last a lifetime; I would not add to her pain. My objective was to keep clear of this atrocious battle and allow the matter to be resolved in a court of law without me. But that was wishful thinking on my part.

I was working at Billingsley's Restaurant in the Van Nuys Golf Course when I received my summons to appear in court. It was just an ordinary day with me sweating under a tall white hat while watching steaks hiss at each other as they turned from blush to black. Across from the smoldering steak broiler was a window where Bonnie sold hot dogs and soda to gluttonous golfers who'd be unfit for any other sport, save maybe bowling. It was from the weenie window that the peculiar gentleman waved to me. "Hi, I'm Lou Callahan," he grinned. "You must be Terry!" I was quite puzzled as to how this complete stranger knew me.

"I'm a friend of your mother's," the sly fox continued as he held out a suspicious envelop, "She told me to give this to you." Believing this cunning little tool I went over to the window and retrieved the envelope from his crooked hand. "You've been served!" he snarled before slipping away like a frightened weasel.

It was my father's close friend and attorney, George Khalua, who had me subpoenaed. My brother also received a 'sham o-gram' from one too cowardly to identify himself. Perhaps this kind of deception is standard practice for criminal lawyers like Khalua but I didn't ever expect to be suckered by someone representing my own dad. Nevertheless, I was called to testify on my father's behalf. His defense was that Rick and I had been gainfully employed and financially self-sufficient since we were fourteen years old, which should have negated any need for an otherwise well-to-do father to support his offspring. Yeah, I don't follow the logic either but that's what you end up with when you have a criminal lawyer handling family matters. Those like Khalua think dads are off the hook as soon as pee-wee opens a lemonade stand.

Three weeks and two depositions later Rick and I found ourselves in a L.A. County courtroom waiting for the case of Michaels vs. Harmon to be heard. After hours of sitting around and doing nothing I was losing my patience. It wasn't until later that afternoon the judge announced that our case would be rescheduled for the following week. I wasn't going to go through another day of this nonsense. After expressing these views to Rick quite audibly, lady justice caught wind of my intentions. "Will Rick Michaels and Terry Michaels please rise." she instructed us. We both stood fast to our feet. "You are both hereby ordered by this court to reappear on..." I don't remember the specific date but I do remember responding with a loud, *"NO WAY!"* Then I attempted to make a mad dash for the door. However, the marshal quickly grabbed hold of my bony arm and dragged me back inside to face the revered woman in the long gothic robe. "Young fellow, sit right here in front of me," the judge demanded. I sat on a hard wooden seat for the longest fifteen minutes of my life then she finally released me with a motherly scolding.

Mom's lawyer told me I got off easy as I could have easily been held for contempt of court. That is certainly what I deserved but instead I received mercy. Experiences like this have helped me to better understand how God operates. When Jesus is our advocate, God doesn't throw the book at us when we break the rules. He shows compassion and offers mercy. He withholds what we really deserve.

Realizing that it was in my own best interest to cooperate with the court order I showed up at the courthouse the following week. Rick and I were wandering the halls when we stumbled upon our ill-fated father who was seated upon a lonely bench. It was awkward for all of us to meet under such unfortunate circumstances but we each managed to keep things on the up and up.

"So, Rick," Dad addressed my brother with a hearty smile, "Do you have any career goals?"
"I like cars." he responded. "I'm thinking about auto mechanics."
"Have you ever thought about broadcasting?" Dad gleamed.
"No," Rick shook his head, "I haven't really given that any thought at all."
"Well, you should consider it." Dad suggested. "If you ever decide to get into radio I'll help you break into the business."

Though Rick had no interest whatsoever in broadcasting I did give the idea consideration. I don't know if it appealed to me because I was sick of slaving over hot grills or perhaps I saw an opportunity as a shoe-in in a potentially lucrative business. Maybe I just wanted to win my father's approval. Whatever the reason might have been, I stood there next to Rick with bated breath waiting for Dad to ask me if I had any career goals. The words were piling fast upon my tongue. "Yes Dad," I'd answer, "Why, I want to go into radio!!!" He never asked me, but the seed was planted.

Following our brief conversation with Dad we filed into the courtroom and waited for our case to be heard. Instead of the nice lady judge who reprimanded me the week before there was a crotchety old gentleman residing on the bench. Mom's attorney was quite pleased to see him as he knew well of his reputation concerning domestic suits. This judge had proven himself to be very unsympathetic toward fathers who fail to support their children. As it turned out Rick and I were not allowed to be part of the proceedings as the wise old judge did not see our relevance to the case. I was flabbergasted that someone finally saw things my way, the judge no less! In the end Mom won the case, Dad remained in Newport Beach with his family and I went on to pursue a career in radio. I visited my father a few weeks after the lawsuit to share with him my intentions. He recommended a good broadcasting school but offered no promises to help me.

*   *   *   *   *

I cannot help but wonder how many happy childhood memories I would have if so many of them had not sunk on the Bon Michel. Sadly, it is far too painful for me to ever climb aboard that boat again. It is as if a part of me is forever lost at sea, a

111

once blue sea that has since become murky and polluted with disturbing images. Pornography is often referred to as a victimless crime. My story tells otherwise. I have seen firsthand the destructive power of porn. It had a horrible hold on my father. It left my mother devastated. It tossed me into a sea of sorrow and confusion. In short, porn took down my entire family. The things that pornography has stolen from me can never be reclaimed. They are gone for good. The devastation that pornography has caused to my family is, perhaps, greater than I'll ever fully realize. Obviously it contributed to my parents splitting and my mother's heartbreak. Yet I also sense that many of my family's dysfunctions, insecurities and anger issues were splatter affects from my father's involvement in porn. It would be a stretch to say that porn was the sole cause of all our issues but I'm dead certain it played a major role.

If you are struggling with porn I bid you to stop. Stop before you sink. Stop before you take others down with you. Stop before you lose all that is precious. Call out to Jesus, He will help you. He will help you even if you've already gone overboard. Take His hand, He'll pull you out. He will save you just as He has saved me. Today I have a new *Bon Michel*. *Bon* is French for 'good'. *Michel* is a biblical name that literally translates to 'Who is like God?' That's Jesus! He is good! He is God! And there is no one else like Him. As for me, I'm now on board with the Lord. He has given me something more precious than childhood memories. He has given me a bright new future, one that is eternal. To that I say, "Bon Michel!"

Chapter 21

GETTING AWAY WITH MURDER

The reason I took Roxanne to get an abortion for the second time was because it was so easy the first time. That is the scary reality about terminating a pregnancy, it's pathetically hassle free. So long as you can completely disassociate yourself from the fact that that little swimmer is a living being it's as simple as putting a rabid dog down. You don't even have to be the one pulling the trigger. All one need do is offer her belly up for target practice and a long line of trigger-happy volunteers will start polishing their pistols. It is not my intent to come off as harsh toward those who have undergone this most unfortunate procedure. I have walked this road myself to a certain degree, and if the shoe were on the other foot it would have been my tummy on the table and not Roxanne's. But the fact that abortion is quick and convenient does not change the cold reality that a brutal act is committed. I also think there would be fewer abortions if young people were truly aware of what they were ridding themselves of. Sadly, though, abortion is pimped off as a quick fix to a common bother no worse than a flea bite.

It wasn't until my wife was pregnant with our first child that I fully grasped how horrific the act of abortion is. We had gone in for an ultrasound while Christy was still in her first trimester. As Dr. Munson swept her hand across my brides slippery belly a wee figure appeared on the small monitor. She had tiny little hands and tiny little feet, and a tiny little heart that went 'beep, beep, beep'. Though our sweet baby was miniature in size everything was there to qualify her as a living, feeling human being. A couple of things happened to me when that tiny person introduced herself onto the screen. Firstly, I celebrated life! I rejoiced over the beautiful new creation formed in Christy's womb. But then it struck me, I was responsible for the murder of two others just like her.

*   *   *   *   *

The funny thing about being young is that statistics get blown way out of proportion especially with regard to sex, and even more so when you factor yourself into the equation. The hormonal teen calculates the chances of pregnancy at one in a billion. If you're wearing a condom the chances improve in your favor to one in a trillion. When passion takes over you're estimating that your sperm has about as much chance at fertilization as a small ice cube on a hot griddle. But, if it just so happens that you wind up as one of those unlikely statistics, there is always the Free Clinic. And once you've walked their red carpet you are no longer worried about statistics at all.

Like any other sixteen year old girl would be, Roxanne was frightened when she suspected that she might be with child. We were already familiar with the Free Clinic and didn't think twice about visiting there. No appointment was made. We just showed up as walk-ins were more than welcome. The waiting room was full but still. Expressions of shame swept across each face. I suspect they all felt dirty as I did. It's one of those places you pray not to bump into a friend or an acquaintance. You don't even want to be spotted by the mailman or local grocery clerk. There are only two reasons why one might end up at a clinic like this, either you're pregnant or you have some embarrassing venereal disease. If a guy shows up alone he's had; the girls know right away that he's not dating material. The Free Clinic is not a social environment even though it might be a common interest that brings like-people together. You're keeping clear from those you suspect might carry the crabs and you're wondering if they're avoiding you for the same reason.

Though we would not have cared to admit it at the time, Roxanne and I did have much in common with the other patients at the clinic. We were all young, confused and scared. We had all gotten ourselves into a predicament for which adolescence had failed to prepare us. We were all afraid of being found out. And, as far as any of us could tell, there was really only one place to run to. The hopelessness one feels in a place such as this is very real. It is felt when sitting next to a thirteen-year-old with a neck full of hickeys. It is felt by the fifteen-year-old who has no one beside her at all. Sadly, there is a segment of Christian society that has waged war against these desperate teens. They, too, are misguided. The issue is not with these lost kids. It is with those who claim to be helping them, the abortionists.

Once the pregnancy was confirmed, Roxanne received counsel should you wish to call it that. If it could truly be considered counsel at all I would not classify it as wise by any stretch of the imagination. The option of going full term was raised but only for the sake of talking us out of it. It was considered a foolish idea which would offer no real benefit to anyone. Abortion was presented as the most viable alternative for our 'little predicament'. It was described as a simple procedure which would be performed in complete secrecy; not even our parents had to know about it. The best news of all was that Uncle Sam would take care of the entire tab. Tell me if that's not a carrot on a stick for a frightened teen? It didn't take long to convince us that this was the most practical way to go. It offered every convenience we could possibly hope for. '*A little bit of suction and the problem goes away? Just show us where to sign!*'

Never did Roxanne or I consider the growth inside her womb as

115

a living being. The thought didn't even cross our minds. I confess we were both quite ignorant of the facts of life and, looking back, it seems that the Free Clinic took willful advantage of our naiveté. Our lack of understanding coupled with the counsel we received led us to believe that abortion wasn't any different than removing an egg from the nest of a chicken. We never thought in terms of a living creature with tiny hands and cute little feet or a precious heart that beats out the sound of life. It did not dawn on us that a soul with unique personality, intellect and emotions had already been formed by the hand of an Almighty Creator. We thought of one thing and one thing only: what's the easiest way out of this situation? How can we stop it before it grows worse? Had we seen a picture of one of these dear babes, an ultrasound image or even a sketch drawing, we would have had other considerations, ones that may have spared a life. But, to us, this growth had more of parasitical nature than a human one. Therefore, we thought only in terms of eradicating it before it became a bigger drain. So, with my full support, Roxanne signed on the dotted line.

*　　*　　*　　*　　*

All went smoothly as promised: the abortion was quick and simple, Uncle Sam popped for all the expenses and no one ever found out. The Free Clinic lived up to its name, ridding the world of one more unwanted pregnancy at no cost to a vulnerable, naïve teenager. They are a dear friend to anyone who can't face the responsibility of their actions. Pass it on to them and they will quickly see to it that it's terminated once and for all. All that's required is that you close your eyes to the sanctity of life. If you can pull that off everything will go without a hitch. Furthermore, you are always welcome back to the clinic should you find yourself in a pickle again. Roxanne and I made a return visit and the second time was easier than the first.

*   *   *   *   *

Since coming to Christ I have had to face a disturbing reality, there is blood on my hands. I not only consented to killing two dear babes that I fathered, I fully encouraged it. If man has been given the supreme authority to determine when life begins then I've done no wrong. But if there is a Creator then He reserves the right to make that determination. And if our Creator determines that life begins at conception then what I have done is outright murder. I can't whitewash it a way. I do believe there is a God and because He is the Author of life and the supreme authority over life, I am guilty of taking a life. Not just one but two, two precious lives He designed before time began and formed in the womb of His choosing. The good news is my bloody hands have been washed by the blood of His hands. The Creator of life entered our world through the womb of a teenaged mother and was born in a humble stall. This child, Jesus, grew in wisdom and in stature and, in His young thirties, took the sins of the world with Him to His death on the cross. The blood on my hands was cleansed when blood poured forth from His. Because of His blood I have been pardoned of murder and every other sin I've committed. Because I've been pardoned I now have the hope of heaven. There I will meet the two children that my selfishness and ignorance robbed from me.

Chapter 22

LAMB THAT WAS SLAIN

I did not quit working at Billingsley's Restaurant because I was treated poorly. In all fairness my boss Drew was pretty good to me. It was the way he treated his wife, Cheryl, which I found disturbing. They were going through a bitter divorce and would get into some ugly, knock-down, drag-out fights right there in the restaurant. Cheryl would swing by, they'd get into it and he'd end up dragging her out by the hair for all to see. Every step of the way Drew would be screaming his fuming head off while she'd be in complete tears. After watching what my own mother went through I couldn't bear to witness any more domestic drama. Besides, I had enough going on in my own household. So I hired on at the Summerhouse Restaurant in Woodland Hills. Come to find out, that's where Drew's ex-wife was employed as a waitress.

The Summerhouse was unique in that it really looked like an authentic summerhouse. Go figure, huh? Plants of all shapes and sizes grew wild from wall to wall inside of the large, two-story dining area. There was so much foliage in the restaurant a young lady came twice a week to care for it all. She was a Panamanian beauty and all the lovesick busboys would follow her from philodendra to philodendra to help hold her ladder. The dishwashers would also crawl out of their cage to gaze upon the voluptuous vine vamp all the while sighing, *"Aye-aye-aye!"* I understood '*Aye-aye-aye*' but didn't understand much else the dishwashers said. Gordo and Miguel came from Jalisco and spoke very little English. My Spanish wasn't any better but I did pick up on a few choice words which won't be repeated. However, I do confess to having used these distasteful terms quite freely with my Mexican friends.

Miguel was a little guy who, along with washing dishes, had the daily task of soaking lettuce heads in a solution which bleached out any bruises on the leaves and kept them crisp. I don't know if this is still practiced today but it was quite common back then. Because Miguel was always flapping around in a large sink of water I called him Sapo (frog). Gordo, on the other hand, was not so little. As the name suggests he was a large fella' and was tall as he was wide. I will not divulge how I referred to Gordo or this manuscript will never make it on Christian bookstands. Why I picked on Gordo and Miguel I do not know; they were always respectful to me. Perhaps I thought I was better than them because I prepared Mediterranean Bouillabaisse while they scraped scum off pots and pans. Or maybe I thought I was a notch above because I was in the country legally and they were Mojados. Whatever my objections were to these two being in 'my' country, or how they got here, they did not justify my poor treatment of them. Mojados or not, Gordo and Miguel were kind gentlemen. I, on the other hand, was not.

Each day I would carry my stack of scummy kitchen wares back to the dishwashing area and yell to Gordo, "*El bleepity-bleepo*". Gordo would respond by saying, "*No mas El bleepity-bleepo, amigo!*" But I would not honor his polite request. I suppose it was my way of letting him know that I was more important than him. But thinking on this, I never would have said '*El bleepity-bleepo*' to Nacho or any of my menacing neighbors in North Hollywood. Nor would I ever have said '*El bleepity-bleepo*' to the Latrine-o Gang at Lanark Park. But Gordo wasn't a cholo or a gang-banger. He wasn't the type to sneak out in the dark and spray '*Viva La Raza*' on the Post Office wall. Gordo was just a family man trying to make a buck, which made me think I could get away with razzing him. So, coward that I was, I continued to greet him with my degrading salutation. And he would promptly reply, *"No mas El bleepity-bleepo, amigo."*

Gordo finally had about all of me he could take. One day after greeting him with my obscene pleasantry he issued a stern warning followed by a look that meant business. "No mas!" he growled, "One more time and..." I understood that much but didn't catch what followed, nor did I even care. *"El bleepity-bleepo, Gordo!"* I repeated. *"El bleepity-bleepo!"* I should have taken Gordo's warning a little more seriously. He charged at me like an angry bull, heaped my frail body over his big, round shoulder then carried me right out the backdoor. With the entire kitchen staff marching behind him Gordo led the way to a dumpster reeking of raw refuse. As he held me over the smelly garbage he gave me one more opportunity to repent before tossing me in. *"No mas El bleepity-bleepo, okay Terry?"* Gordo fumed. *"Okay, Gordo,"* I surrendered, *"No mas!"* He quickly released me and we shook on it.

After my close encounter of the putrid kind I gained a new appreciation for Gordo. Never did I address him in a derogatory manner again. Just to be fair I even quit calling Miguel 'Sapo'. Before long I established a close camaraderie with all the Mexicanos at The Summerhouse. We worked through the language barrier and spoke to one another in the universal language of respect. I would go so far as to say they embraced me as one of their own calling me 'hermano'. Gordo, who loved to sing loudly while he labored, grew especially kind toward me. He taught me a few Spanish songs like 'Eres Tu' and 'Una Paloma Blanca'. To this day I still remember most the words to 'La Bamba' thanks to Gordo.

Though we established a cordial working relationship we never really socialized outside of The Summerhouse until one day

121

Gordo invited me to his home for dinner. The invitation was extended to many others but the only gringos asked to come were me and another cook named Dave. Initially I had reservations about attending; I don't think I would have gone it alone. But since Dave was going that took some of the edge off, so I rode out with him.

By the time we arrived at Gordo's the house was already packed with people. All the guests were male and all were Spanish speaking, with the exception of the lone gringos who must have stood out like two snow rabbits in an alligator farm. Not only were Dave and I white we were *very, very white.* Neither of us could pass for Mexicans if we hid under large sombreros and long ponchos. Both of us had pale faces and long blonde hair, his dishwater and mine platinum. Not knowing many of the guests we had some pause as to whether all would be on board the welcome wagon for a couple of Anglos. Our fears were soon put to rest once we were led into the kitchen. Piping hot tortillas were tossed to us as fast as they could come off the fire.

For those who may not know this, butchering livestock in the suburbs of L.A. is generally prohibited in residential areas. Should this be a new revelation to you, you are not alone. Gordo never got the memo either. It happened right in his backyard; a lamb was slain. This is true; I'm not pulling the wool over your eyes! A lamb was slaughtered and the fat of it was prepared for all to partake of. Chunks of fresh meat stewed in a large pot, filling the entire house with a flavorful aroma. Before long we were stuffing our tortillas with tender strips carved from a common carcass. As we shared the sacrificial lamb I sensed a spirit of oneness within a mixed group where prejudice too often divides. But this evening was about communion. It mattered not which side of the border one was from; we were 'todos hermanos' as we shared in the lamb which was slain.

As I reflect back upon this experience I am reminded of the church in its infancy. In the second chapter of Acts we read how the believers of the very first church were always together and had all things in common. (See Acts 2:44) They really didn't have all that much in common outwardly but their hearts were knit together by the Lamb that was slain. We are also told that these early Christian pioneers *continued daily with one accord*, they *broke bread from house to house* and together *they ate their food with gladness and simplicity of heart*. You can see this for yourself in Acts 2:46. In the very next verse you'll notice how God added to the fellowship daily. This was a happy group which people longed to be part of. There was acceptance. There was togetherness. There was gladness. There was even food!

It wasn't long, though, before things got a little messy in the family of God. Jump up four chapters from Acts 2 to Acts 6 and you land the midst of a squabble, the first in church history as far as the record shows. The conflict erupted at the dinner fellowship and had to do with ethnicity. The 'illegals' felt that the widows of the natural citizens were given higher priority in the food line. This was quickly corrected when (judging by their names) seven 'illegals' were recruited to oversee the meal ministry. Once spatulas were placed in their willing and able hands the church took off again and it grew exponentially (See Acts 6:7). The lesson is this; before the church *got it together* the people had to *get together* and unite as one.

The Apostle Paul also told the Corinthian church to get it together as the family there was divided over the most stupid things. "We follow Peter, the brawny fisherman!" some said. "Paul, the Pharisee turned Jesus freak, is our man!" another group exclaimed. "That's nothing," declared group three, "We hang onto every word of the great orator Apollos. "Oh, yeah," the fourth group boasted, "We've got y'all beat! We're totally

123

into Jesus!" Nowhere were their differences more apparent than at (you guessed it) the supper table. Read all about it in 1 Corinthians 11:17-22. It's horrifying! Paul told them, *"You come together not for the better but for the worse."* How does this kind of ugliness creep into the house of the Lord? It happens when we get our eyes off the one thing we all have in common only to focus on our differences whether they are doctrinal, political or racial or anything else. It is probably true, in the outside world most of us would have little to do with each other. We are distinctly different from one another. But in the House of God we all have one precious thing in common, the Lamb that was slain.

Chapter 23

ONE SYLLABLE AT A TIME
A Nun See Eight

I enrolled at the Don Martin School of Communications in Hollywood for two reasons. For one, my father recommended it. Reason two, many of my favorite radio personalities had attended this prestigious learning institution. Don Martin's offered a twelve month program for aspiring disc jockeys which included spinning records, console operation, news delivery, commercial writing and production. They even helped with job placement. Evening classes met Monday through Friday from six o 'clock to ten o'clock. I really had to hustle to make it there on time as my shift at The Summerhouse ended at four. Then I'd have to suck exhaust in bumper-to-bumper traffic as I drove from Topanga Canyon in Canoga Park all the way to Hollywood Boulevard. Thankfully, it was just enough time for the smell of grilled sirloin to wear off.

All my instructors at Don Martin's were seasoned veterans in the business. Everyone loved the big Okie, Larry Tomlison, who had worked as a news anchorman in Oklahoma City. Then there was the younger and hipper Bob Leutrell who had deejayed at more than a few pop stations in major market areas. My favorite teacher, though, was a silver haired gentleman named Jack Brown. He always wore a large grin and kept an unlit cigar between his nicotine stained teeth. By day, Mr. Brown served as president of Armed Forces Radio. He had a lot of big guns working under him at the time, air personalities like the legendary Wolfman Jack and the Real Don Steel. This is what I was paying the big bucks for.

It was at Don Martin's that I met up again with Ric Wonders, that big surfer dude who ran the Mustard Seed Coffee House. We sat next to each other in class and became pretty close friends but neither of us talked about Jesus anymore. We just discussed the radio biz and our dreams to make it big one day. Ric longed for a gig in Hawaii doing some kind of surf program. I guess that meant he'd be playing songs like 'Wipe Out' and 'Pipeline' while reporting on wave conditions over the intros. I'm not sure if he ever made it to the island or even into radio for that matter. Or maybe he did catch that wave and is sittin' on top of the world!

Larry Tomlison was the one who taught me how to annunciate, which was no small feat. He claimed I was the only person he'd ever heard who could turn full sentences into just one syllable. It was true; I had a very lazy speech pattern and mumbled most everything. Unless I was degrading people like German auto mechanics or Mexican dishwashers my words were typically all slurred together. Perhaps I had the fear of being understood because I'd generally get my butt beat if I articulated my thoughts too clearly. To break my poor speech habits Larry would have me read news copy very slowly and deliberately while concentrating on each and every syllable one at a time. By the time I grad...u...a...ted in...to the ad... vanced class Mis.. ter Brown won... dered why I spoke like a poor...ly pro...grammed ro...bot. And I was the son of a radio/TV wonder, one with whom all my instructors and many of my classmates were well familiar. The apple didn't fall anywhere near the tree. It didn't even land in the orchard.

There are all kinds of personalities that pursue careers in radio. I met most of them at Don Martin's. Gary Briggs, who was a bit of a mama's boy, was there to overcome an inferiority complex. Then there was the egomaniac Chris Feltman who'd keel over and die if everyone didn't take note of him. Nobody loved Chris like Chris. He'd attempt to go shirtless in class but Larry would stop him and say, "What do you think you're doing?" Rudy Baker was a sports nut. To him radio was a means of getting involved in the game without having to stay in shape. We even had a pimp in our class who worked the same block the school was located on. He had one of those smooth voices like Don Cornelius of *Soul Train* fame. A few party animals attended Don Martin's to live out some kind of rock 'n roll fantasy. And we had a couple of older guys working their way through midlife crises and trying to find themselves. Then there was me. It wasn't a love, it wasn't a passion. For me, radio offered the path of least resistance. I saw it as an easy field to break into because of my heritage.

I learned very quickly that radio wasn't all about personality. There was a lot of skill involved too. It wasn't like today where all the music and commercials are digitally pre-programmed. Deejays had to know their stuff and they had to be fast. You had two turntables to alternate back and forth from for playing records (those flat black vinyl things). Then you had a multi-layer cartridge machine for airing commercials which were pre-recorded on something that looked like an eight-track. Most spots were either thirty or sixty seconds long and the average record in the seventies was about three to three and a half minutes. So your hands were constantly moving pressing buttons, turning knobs and queuing up song intros.

Deejays also needed to know how to mix music. This was the real art, segueing from one song to the next so the listener couldn't tell when the last one ended and the next one began. Finally you needed to know what kind of record intros you were dealing with. Some had a music bed of six seconds while others could be as long as twenty. Whatever length it was that was all the time you had to do your rap. Stepping on vocals was one unpardonable sin in radio. The other was dead air. That's why deejays had to have some basic math skills. If you only had nine minutes and thirty seconds until the top of the hour your next three songs better add up to exactly that. You don't want to come up short nor do you want to interrupt someone's favorite tune. Timing had to be precise.

Once we were trained in each of these skills the final project was to put together a demo tape. This is where we did an actual show in the broadcast studio spinning records, speaking over intros and delivering news, sports and weather. This demo would also include a self-produced commercial with music and sound effects spliced into it. All this was done on a massive reel-to-reel Ampex recorder which was about as big as a kitchen range. If I remember right, we spent a couple months producing demos until we came up with one we were pleased with. I could have used a few additional months as my final product was kind of shaky. But I was in a hurry. A few weeks prior to graduation Larry passed a job lead onto me in Fort Bragg, California. It was the first demo I ever sent out and I got a call back the following week. They needed someone to start immediately, so within a few short days I found myself waving good-bye to L.A. My diploma from Don Martin's had to be mailed to me as I graduated earlier than the rest of my class.

I look back on my experience at Don Martin's and see how God used it to prepare me for what I do now as a Bible teacher. Obviously, I needed a lot of help with my speaking skills. Not that all preachers need radio voices but it does help if you can understand what they are saying. Quite honestly, if I'm forced to listen to some miserable monotone minister mumble his way through Malachi for an hour I'm probably going to conk out on whoever's shoulder is next to me. And they probably won't mind because the entire pew will be falling on each other's shoulders like dominoes. So, I for one am grateful that I was taught to articulate and annunciate. It is important for me that the gospel message is well communicated and clearly understood. I think the Lord would prefer it that way too.

Another thing I learned in broadcasting school was that effective communicators stick to the point. This is especially true with commercial copy. When you've got sixty seconds to sell an idea you don't have the luxury of bunny trailing into other irrelevant subject matter. If you're going to talk about bath soap you don't bring up shoelaces or vegetable oil. The same goes for delivering the news. You can't just go off on tangents, you stick to the story. For example, it would not be a good time to announce the birth of a two-headed turtle in Tallahassee when covering the Middle East conflict. If you go off into too many directions people just get lost or think you're schizo. These are principles I continue to apply to my pulpit ministry. Rather than overwhelm people with multiple ideas I focus on one main theme so no one leaves feeling like their head just got off the heavy-duty spin cycle.

The important thing I want to convey to the reader is how God prepared me to be used of Him. Even as I worked in kitchens He was equipping me for the role of a minister. Cooking taught me important lessons in the area of service. Basically, that's what ministry is all about. In a word it's 'service'. Perhaps you're at a place where you're wondering what the Lord has in store for you. Maybe you even feel frustrated with where you're at. Please consider that God is preparing you for something special. He longs to use you in ways you never even imagined. I encourage you to be faithful where He has placed you and remain teachable. See what God does. Listen to His voice. Don't step on His vocals. Don't allow for any dead air. God is going to produce something awesome, believe me.

Chapter 24

THE BIG GIG

There are things which a demo tape fails to reveal about a person. While they may be effective in demonstrating voice quality and technical skills they don't reveal much about one's character. Physical appearance would be another trait which electro-magnetic reproduction hides very well. There are a lot of shady people who would never get hired if audiotape divulged such secrets and I'm quite certain I would have been numbered among them. I was probably doomed from the start when I joined on at KDAC. Once the general manager got a good look at me my chances of longevity were less than a mayfly's. Maybe I should have gotten a haircut before leaving L.A. Perhaps I should have never worn tattered 501 blues and a scrappy T-shirt at our initial introduction. But that's who I was and I saw no reason to put on false pretenses. Besides, someone once told me I had the perfect face for radio.

If my sloppy appearance didn't stack the deck against me I'm sure my questionable character did. After all I was shacking up with a girl, not jus any girl... a black girl! *An underage black girl!* As far as I could tell she was the only African American in all of Fort Bragg at the time. At least I never saw any others. And I know for certain she was the only African American attending Fort Bragg High School where we enrolled her as a senior. Roxanne was not the most popular girl in school as you might imagine. She really didn't make any friends there at all. And because Roxanne dressed rather racy she also drew a lot of scrutiny from her teachers. But what were they to do, send her home with a note?

Aside from the scandal we brought to this sleepy town Fort Bragg was absolutely gorgeous. It is nestled on the picturesque Mendocino Coast in Northern California where giant redwoods collide with majestic ocean bluffs. Not only was Fort Bragg home to the many lumberjacks and fishermen who settled there, sea lions also preferred the cool sea air as they clustered upon slippery, wet rocks on the lower shore. From the bridge on Highway 1 you could watch old wooden fishing vessels float off into the misty morning sea from Noyo Harbor or you could wait for nightfall when they returned with their catch. Even back in the seventies this historic township took one back forty years. The tiny business district had all the charm and nostalgia of Mayberry and the homes also maintained an old fashioned flavor.

Fort Bragg was a simple town and her people preferred it that way. They were hardworking, conservative folks who held to traditional values. Women kept the home while their men cast nets at sea or cut timber for Georgia Pacific. This was a city where folks respected the law and saw the value of town hall meetings. There was community involvement, a volunteer fire department and local parades to celebrate legendary figures like Paul Bunyan. Saturday nights were for burping beer in Noyo Harbor's tavern. Sunday mornings were set aside for that old time religion. You either fit the mold or you didn't belong. As for Roxanne and I, we didn't blend in too well.

As clean cut as Gary Briggs was he might have survived in this circumspect city. He was recruited by KDAC shortly after I was. Being a mama's boy, though, Gary couldn't stand the idea of being so far from home and went back after just one day. The egomaniac Chris Feltman came fast on his heels as a quick replacement. While he may have been guilty of conceit he didn't have all the baggage that might bring shame to his fellow man. Then there was Wayne Wilcox who joined the team at KDAC shortly after Chris came aboard. Wayne was a longhair like me who somehow managed to fly under the radar in spite of his sordid lifestyle. His girlfriend, Lucy, employed herself as a streetwalker in San Francisco. All the jocks knew she was a hooker but that secret was good with us. Finally, there was Ferrell who hired on as a part-time jock. He was quite a bit older than the rest of us, probably in his upper forties. His big pot belly, bald noggin and wiry whiskers gave him an air of maturity but in reality Ferrell was the most childish of us all. We only put up with him because he was the guy with the weed.

KDAC was a mom 'n pop operation. The owner, Charles Granite, also served as general manager. At least that's what he wanted us to believe. The one who really ran the show, though, was his wife Betty. While Charles wanted things done a certain way Betty demanded another. This made it virtually impossible for the jocks to stay out of trouble. If you followed Charles' directions you were bound to get an angry call from the missus. We never saw her around the station much but each of us averaged about ten calls per shift from her. If that weren't enough to create havoc our program director, Dave Granite, was the son of this conflicted couple. Naturally, he had his own ideas as to how things ought to be run. Needless to say, the jocks were always getting chewed out for something. Because it was a lose-lose proposition I decided to do things my way.

Along with being the program director Dave was also the music director. This meant that he approved all the songs on the play list. When 'You Are the Sunshine of My Life' by Stevie Wonder was added I was the first to air it. Because I was the first to air this mega-hit I also became the first to get my butt chewed over it. Charles darted into the studio yelling, *"Get*

133

that screaming nigger sh*# off the radio right now!!!"
I can only surmise that Charles may have been Afro-phobic.
This was further confirmed the day I gave Roxanne a brief tour
of the facilities. Shortly after she left Charles came in sneering,
"I can tell you girlfriend was here. Those coloreds have a certain
smell about them." But the only stench I detected in the room
was the foul odor of an ignorant mind.

It wasn't just Charles; the entire Granite family was as racist as
could be. Yet they faithfully attended church every Sunday to
worship a Jesus created in their own Anglo image. And as they
left the holy sanctuary, thankful to God for their pure vanilla
epidermises, Betty would call me at the station to request a
Sunday morning gospel song. Theirs was an ugly form of
Christianity which totally repulsed me. Though I may have been
far from Jesus I knew Him well enough to realize He wasn't
some whitey. I also understood that the cross wasn't just for
those with fair complexions but it represented God's love for the
whole world. I don't know what kind of Bible the Granite's
read. My best guess is that it probably had a pale cover and the
page with John 3:16 was most likely blacked out... or maybe they
used White Out.

It is not my intent to paint the Granite's as the villains in my
story that I might be portrayed as the innocent victim. The truth
is my life was a total mess and I was sinking fast and furiously.
As true as that may be I saw no salvation on that boat the
Granite's were on. It was a battleship fighting a losing war against
God's own beautiful creation, yet a Christian flag waved high
upon its Arian mast. As for me, I couldn't get on board with a
form of Christianity which promoted hatred or sizing people up
by the color of their skin. Perhaps what scared me most was that
I saw a little bit of my old self in the Granite's - that pre-
dumpster punk who would degrade illegals who sought only a

meager morsel of the American Dream. This is not a statement on immigration. I'm just saying we shouldn't hate people under any circumstances.

What I experienced at KDAC was pure unadulterated hatred; I don't know any other way to express it. Even those things to my credit were used as ammunition against me. The Granite's were very familiar with the legacy left by my father at KGO, the ABC affiliate in San Francisco. As a pioneer in shock radio during the sixties Clete Harmon became a household name throughout the Bay Area. This only lent to high expectations of me by the Granite's which I never measured up to. I was once told by Dave, "Your dad is Clete Harmon, you have a First Class Radio License and you can't even wipe your _ _ _ with it!" While it was true my skills were not up to par I only saw his comments as seepage from the raw sewer of a cold heart.

I fully expected my first job in radio to be difficult. I understood that there would be challenges which I would have to rise up to as a rookie in the business. Don Martin's had sufficiently prepared all of us for such things. But the cruelty I experienced at KDAC caught me totally off guard. The fact that the Granite's were church going people made it even more appalling. I guess that's the real rub for me. Not to say that I was any better but when I was a pig to the Hoffman's or to Gordo I didn't drag Jesus into it. If my understanding is correct, this is what it means to take the Lord's name in vain. And when one professes Christ while at the same time promotes hatred - His body takes the hit. The church is no longer perceived as something glorious but, rather, as something altogether repulsive.

Pride and prejudice might make for a fantastic recipe for a Hollywood screenplay but such traits are hazardous to the church. They reduce it to an elite club where the doors remain closed to the very people God longs to reach. Christianity and bigotry are on total opposite ends of the spectrum, the two can never be reconciled. One is all about love, acceptance and unity while the other represents hostility, rejection and division. We're not just talkin' apples and oranges here. It is the difference between light and darkness. Christianity is a celebration of the regenerated life while bigotry immortalizes the degenerated life.

This is not to say that bigots can't ever change but it does require an act of God for that to happen, just like caterpillars can't fly unless God radically transforms them into those pretty winged creatures called butterflies. Until that occurs they just crawl around with their noses in the dirt. However, a butterfly won't stoop that low. As a new creature she soars to wonderful new heights, viewing creation from a grander perspective. Bigots are a lot like caterpillars. They appear fuzzy to one another but their noses are entrenched in dirt. Wearing Christianity as a religion won't change them it only highlights their filth and makes it uglier. What is needed is a complete transformation to get them out of the grime. This is something only God can do. And when bigots become butterflies their dirt no longer sticks behind.

Chapter 25

YER KIND AIN'T WELCOME

Because there was such a serious housing shortage in Fort Bragg the best living accommodations I could find was a Silver Stream aluminum trailer. This modest sized fifth-wheel sat in a quaint mobile home park near the ocean bluff and rented for about eighty bucks a month. Quarters were so cramped in this tin shell there wasn't adequate space for even a small shower stall. The good news was there were showering facilities on grounds, just a few short steps from our trailer space. The bad news was - no hot water! Because the water was so blasted freezing I'd generally get my bathing finished in less than a minute flat. Thankfully, after about a month of this nonsense, Chris scored a double-wide in the same park where Roxanne and I lived. He was kind enough to let us shower at his place on a daily basis.

While Chris' double-wide became a bath and beauty spa by day it was my Silver Stream rental that became 'party central' by night. Chris, Wayne and Ferrell would cluster around my confined living space with Roxanne and me, and we'd all get wasted together. Things would get especially crazy on the weekends when we'd stay up late to watch *Saturday Night Live*. Evidently the thin aluminum walls were not sufficient to muffle our loud and hysterical chatter. I know this to be true because one morning I found a note on our door which affirmed this fact. This brief note also stated that we had exactly three days to vacate the premises and it was signed '*management*'.

Our eviction notice left me in quite a panic as I was very doubtful we'd ever find another place in the area to live. I immediately went to Priscilla, the on-grounds manager, and pleaded with her to reconsider things. Unfortunately it was out of her hands as the decision to evict us had been made by Mr. Gentry, the park owner. Being sympathetic to my plight, however, Priscilla passed onto me Mr. Gentry's home address so I could appeal to him in person.

Roxanne and I wasted no time and went straight over to Mr. Gentry's. He was a tall, silver haired cuss and his large frame filled the entire doorway. Ol' Gentry wore an ugly scowl on his face, one which told me he wasn't too excited about our visit. Regardless of the cold reception I pleaded with this huge man as if I were pleading for my own life. I promised that we would never entertain guests at the trailer again. I swore that the TV volume would be kept down to a minimum then turned off by nine o'clock sharp. I gave my solemn word that the neighbors would never hear another peep from us. But the heartless giant just stood there quietly with that nasty scowl on his face while he peered down on us with two squinting eyes.

After a long moment of silence Mr. Gentry muttered, "Yer kind ain't welcome 'round here." *'What kind did he mean?'* I wondered. *'The black kind? The hippy kind? The nigger lover kind?'* What did it matter? Prejudice however you slice it still comes out the same, it's sick. My only hope was to plead for more time. "Can I get a couple weeks?" I begged. He just shook his head. "A week?" His response was the same. Mr. Gentry showed no mercy, he wanted our kind out immediately.

I called home that evening to get some good motherly counsel. Mom suggested that I go to the Catholic Church as they tended to be quite helpful with such matters. The very next day I found myself at the local parish sharing my dilemma with a kindly man of the cloth. This dear priest was a compassionate fellow with two ready ears willing to soak in my sad story with the sincerest of interest. As it turned out, a nun from his parish had recently moved leaving a vacancy at a nearby apartment. The gracious rector even placed a call to the manager so I could get situated right away. I saw no need to inform him, mind you, that I was shacking up with a girl. Besides, the subject never really came up and I was not willing to volunteer information that might embarrass a holy man such as him. What I'm really trying to say is I didn't think it was any of his business.

It wasn't the nicest apartment complex in town but it sure beat the one in North Hollywood where thugs did thrive. Plus this one had showers, not just one but two! We also had two good sized bedrooms. The second one we ended up renting to Wayne and his girlfriend, Lucy. She was rarely there, though, as she spent most her evenings on the streets of San Francisco hooking.

For the most part our new surroundings were rather peaceful and the neighbors kept to themselves. We did, however, have one incident with the couple across the hall. It seems they had a habit of always banging their door when they got home. One time in the wee hours of the night their door slammed so hard it shook the walls as if a sonic boom went off. We were all up watching TV when the blast occurred and Wayne, who was extremely rattled by the disruption, flew right out of his seat. He quickly retaliated by swinging our entry door wide open then slamming it shut with all his might. Within seconds our rival was pounding on our door yelling, "Open up or I'm breaking in!" We tried to ignore this hostile creature but, true to his word, he made every effort to break our door down by throwing his body against it. We saw no other choice but to comply with the wishes of this raging lunatic. So, Wayne reluctantly welcomed our violent neighbor inside as his supportive wife trailed quietly behind him.

The brawny lumberjack (who obviously drunk his fair share of ale) barged straight into our living room. I openly confess that this boisterous galoot frightened me more than the Chicano gangster, Nacho. You could see the veins bulging from his boiling flesh as he began ranting and cursing at us. He even threatened to kill us! All the while his wife affirmed the idea by bobbing her head like a dashboard Chihuahua.

Roxanne did not take too kindly to our neighbor's cruel disposition and attempted to shout him down. He quickly advanced toward her, threatening to throw her elfin body from our second story balcony. I think he may have actually done it had his wife not interceded. When Wayne told Roxanne to call the sheriff, the angry drunk exclaimed, "Go ahead, he's my brother!" Rather than involve the limp arm of the law we just let the hot head continue to blow his stack and kept our lips zipped. Once he got everything off his burly chest his head-bobbing wife led him out into the cold, dark night. Though this belligerent maniac wasn't very neighborly I suspect Mr. Gentry would have gladly welcomed his kind.

Chapter 26

BLOOPERS

Prior to living in the sticks of Northern California I had never been exposed to small town radio before. I grew up listening to the seasoned pros in major markets like the Bay Area, San Diego, the O.C. and L.A. The jocks who work in these large metropolitan areas are typically slick and polished. Yet they had all paid their dues in some one horse town like Fort Bragg. And they all have stories to tell of how they had to sweep the studio floor, wash windows, buff the microphone or shine up the console. The listener may think you've reached celebrity status but you're really nothing more than a juke box with a feather duster. I wonder if Wolfman Jack would have had the same mystique if people knew he was pushing a broom to '*Heartbreak Hotel*'.

Small town radio can also sound a lot like amateur hour. Mistakes which would be unforgivable in the big city are numerous in the more rural communities. Your only saving grace is that the listeners are quite accustomed to it. And for some, that little crackpot station might be their only point of reference of what real broadcasting is all about. In small town U.S.A. it is not uncommon to hear some bumbling jock trip over his tongue between records, or butcher the news, or introduce Barry Manilow as Willy Nelson. It happens. And back in the day when songs were still recorded on vinyl platters you could hear music segues that resembled the sounds you might hear coming from a train wreck. These rinky-dink stations also put out more dead air than a graveyard. Either the deejay miscalculated in his back timing, got distracted with a phone call or took too long in the bathroom. Maybe you've wondered what jocks do when they have to go. Well, in my day they'd put on 'Macarthur Park'. This was an extremely long song and most jocks I knew didn't even care for the tune. In my humble opinion, the only reason it got as much airplay as it did was it gave deejays ample time to run to the toilet. You can thank our bladders for getting that song on Billboard's Top 40. The album version of 'American Pie' also aided us in the area of potty breaks. If Don Martin's had trained us to hold our pee for four hours Don McClean might never have scored a number one hit with that song.

I had my first blooper the very first day I started at KDAC. To add insult to injury, it happened the very first time I opened up the microphone. All I was supposed to do was give a quick station ID. You would think anyone could pull off a simple assignment such as this. I don't know how I blew it but I did. In all honesty, I thought I had nailed it and had come across like a true veteran of the airwaves. I was certain that my stellar voice had cut through the coastal fog and enchanted its way into the hearts of countless deejay groupies who dreamt under majestic pines while clutching transistor radios tight to their bosoms. I knew they would be begging for more after hearing my smooth and rich voice announce, "KDAC, Los Angeles." But all that pride and fantasy took a nosedive when Dave reminded me, "It's KDAC, *Fort Bragg*!"

This would not be the last of my blunders; there would be a host of others to follow. Generally speaking I'd get hammered every time I read news copy. It seems like I was always mispronouncing important words like 'gubernatorial'. Even though 'goober natural' is a much more amusing way to express such a drab term, my boss wasn't impressed in the least. Reading sports copy proved to be an even bigger catastrophe for me.

Because I never took an interest in competitive games most sports terms were as foreign to me as tuna fish is to Jessica Simpson. However, because I have read my fair share of PGA headlines I now know that a 'bogey' is not to be confused with those irritating little objects found in ones nostrils. When I blew that one the GM really got teed off but... that was par for the course.

For a good while there I was working seven days per week at KDAC. Weekends were especially rough. My shift would end at midnight on Saturday and I'd be back in the saddle on Sunday morning at six sharp. For the first couple hours it was all religious programming. Reverend J. Vernon McGee's program would play off a huge reel-to-reel recorder and after he wrapped up I'd cut live to a local church feed. I had no interest in any either of these broadcasts and, quite honestly, they had a way of lulling my heavy eyelids back to sleep. One time, after finding my face flat on the console, I saw poor McGee's program spinning helplessly off the reel. After a quick glance at the clock I soon realized that I was responsible for ten full minutes of dead air. It seems that everyone else in Fort Bragg was snoozing like I was as not one person ever called to complain.

No doubt, I had my fair share of flubs at KDAC and I'm sure they caused as much disgrace to the station as they did to me. But all my bloopers combined seemed trivial compared to Dave's big blunder. Chris and I were in the broadcast studio while I was doing my show. Through the wide window into the production room we could see Dave trying to pre-record the fish and game report. It was obvious he was getting very frustrated as we watched him rewind the tape time and again to start over. With every take he'd trip over his tongue then fly into a fit of rage and cuss out the walls. Time was running short for Dave and the program was due to go on the air within minutes. After

143

giving it a fifth or sixth whirl Dave got tongue tied again. He had another cussing fit and when he saw Chris and me laughing he flew into the studio to give us a verbal lashing with words unfit for polite society. After calling us every name in the book Dave returned to the studio to record his cheesy little program. He finally got through his read with the next take then quickly queued the tape up for broadcast.

Dave made two crucial mistakes. The first goof was not stopping the recorder when he threw his hissy-fit. The second mistake was not pushing the 'record' button when he did the clean re-take. So when the broadcast went out, which listeners thought to be aired live, everyone on the Mendocino Coast got a shocking surprise. The program began with, "Good afternoon, this is Dave Stone with the KDAC fish and guh... guh, oh *&%#!, *I HATE DOING THIS BULL :?(*&%$##!*" After a host of many foul expletives you could hear two angry feet stomp out of the production room, then Dave could be heard in the studio cussing out Chris and me. It all happened so fast and unexpectedly that there was no time to stop this prerecorded rampage. Every vulgar word you can imagine went out over the public airwaves. As you might already suspect, Dave got torn into pretty bad by his dear old dad. Afterward he told Chris and me, "Just be glad it wasn't you! You would have been fired on the spot!" We knew very well that he was right but that didn't stop us from laughing our heads off. We were in hysterics for days.

*　　*　　*　　*　　*

Bloopers are a fact of life, not just for deejays but for all of us. The only difference is your bloopers aren't broadcast over the public airwaves. Can you imagine if they were? Perhaps I should qualify what a blooper is. First let me state what a blooper isn't.

144

Those sins we commit knowingly and willingly, those are not bloopers. Bloopers are those things you can put an *'oops'* in front of. To say, "Oops, I stole a boom box from Wal-Mart!" doesn't fly very well. Bloopers aren't planned or premeditated, they just happen without any forethought whatsoever. For example, we recently had a Christian rock group come out from California to play at our church. These young guys had never been to Texas before so a couple of them decided to record their trip on video. In their effort to capture a panoramic view of the Texas Hill Country they climbed up a water tower. It wasn't until the police pulled up that they realized they had broken the law. These poor kids spent the night in jail and had to come up with a thousand dollars each for bail money.

Even bloopers have consequences. Just because they weren't planned or premeditated doesn't get us off the hook. We still have to admit guilt and take responsibility for them. Bloopers are also good reminders that it's impossible to keep the law no matter how hard we try. That's why we can't trust laws to save us. The Rabbis and Pharisees made a big mistake by adding more laws on top of God's laws. That only increases blooper potential. What we need is grace that's big enough to cancel out all our bloopers. And that is the kind of grace we have at our disposal through Christ Jesus. He will rewind the entire reel of your life and record 'forgiven' over every last blooper.

145

Chapter 27

WEDDING BELL BLUES
In Memory of a Man I Never Met

"Good afternoon, Terry Michaels with you on the AM dial. You're listening to KDAC, Fort Bragg. Sunshine with occasional high clouds can be expected throughout the day, highs will reach around seventy-two degrees. And now... here's a blast from the past off the request line... The Fifth Dimension..."

"Billl! I love you so, I always will..."

The song was 'Wedding Bell Blues'. It would not be the first time I would play this nostalgic sixties hit nor would it be the last. Everyday it was the same caller with the same request. "Hey Tuh... Tuh... Terry. Cuh... cuh... can you puh... play wuh... wuh... Wedding buh-Bell Blues? Puh... puh... please, Terry?" His name was Bill, just like in the song. Lead singer Marilyn McCoo serenades the man of her dreams, pleading for his hand in marriage. *"Won't you marry me, Billll..."* she belts out with every ounce of passion she can muster. She woos. She charms. She hopes. Things worked out pretty well for the sultry songstress. She did marry... a guy named Bill! He also sang with the Fifth Dimension.

Bill of KDAC request-line fame wasn't so fortunate. He never did marry. He did come close once. Bill and Cindy were sweethearts. She wore his ring. They had gotten engaged and the date was set. Yes, Bill was in love... deeply in love. But Cindy left. She promised she would always be there but... she left. True story. Sad story. Cindy left Bill. She left after the accident; the one that left Bill impaired... brain damaged. It was this very accident that slowed Bill down... way, way down. Bill wasn't the same anymore so Cindy left. Ever since that sorrowful day she said goodbye Bill spent his days calling the request line. As soon as the record ended he would call again. "Cuh... cuh... can you puh-play it one more tuh... tuh... time, tuh-Terry?" he would plead with a stammer, "Puh... puh... please?"

Cindy did what most any other young gal would have done in her situation. After all, things change. Circumstances change. Plans change. People change. Bill changed so Cindy changed her mind. That's just human nature. It keeps the back door open a crack just in case there's a need to slip away. Folks need a quick out in the event of some unforeseen change. Even love comes with a brake pedal. It's there for those sudden stops where turns get risky. We will recite vows openly and publicly but the stipulations remain undisclosed. The strings attached to our promises stay hidden. They only come out should things change. We hope they don't but there is always a contingency plan for if they do. It's buried somewhere in the back of our minds... crumpled up so we never have to look at it... unless, of course, something unexpected comes up.

"Cuh... cuh... can you puh... play it again, Tuh... Terry?" Bill would stutter. "Puh... puh... please?" Usually I wouldn't but sometimes I would. And as soon as the song faded to an end the phone would ring. "Thuh... thanks for puh... playing my song, tuh... tuh... Terry," he politely would tell me, "Cuh... cuh... can I muh... meet you? Puh... please?" I explained to Bill how I had a policy never to meet with listeners. It was true. I adapted that rule when Bill started calling.

Cindy's dream changed but poor Bill's never did. He lived for a song, a memory of what once was, a reminder of what would never be. She left. She left him with dashed hopes and a crushed heart. And everyday Bill would call the request line, at least a dozen times per day, to request the melody that became 'their' song... back when they dreamed together... when love was reckless, wild and in full bloom. I wondered if the 'Wedding Bell Blues' soothed the pain or added to it. But when the bull horns blasted through the fog filled air I suspected that the melody he lived for only added to his sorrows.

The thunderous bull horns could be heard echoing from the coastal bluffs to the majestic pines and throughout the still city. They sounded off only when there was an emergency to alert the fire and rescue volunteers. After that, it was up to us at KDAC to call and get the news release so we could broadcast the story. If it was a suicide attempt by Bill we didn't air it. I suppose we could have by leaving his name out but most would have figured it was him anyway. So we just canned it. Then days would pass and Bill would be calling again, "Cuh... cuh... can you puh... play the wuh... wuh... Wedding Bell Blues? Puh... puh... please?"

*   *   *   *   *

Neither you nor I can really be sure what we would have done had we been in Cindy's shoes. Even what we may call 'unconditional love' has conditions under extreme circumstances. There may be a lot of thick layers over it but there is a threshold within the heart of every person. We can only take so much. I'm neither justifying nor excusing our inadequacies. I'm simply stating they are there. Mankind is imperfect therefore our love is imperfect. We strive for 'agape' but at times it gets sloppy. God is different. He loves us with a perfect love. His love is unchangeable, unstoppable and absolutely unconditional. There is nothing we can ever do to make God change His mind about us. Scripture tells us that He

149

knew us before the foundations of the world. Before time began He saw each of our lives from beginning to end. He saw every flaw, fault and failure. He saw through all the darkness and yet He loved us. With God there are no unforeseen changes that would cause Him to check out. He knew everything up front. Though we may shift like the wind, His love for us never will. It can't. If it could that would make God imperfect but He's not. And because He loves us He keeps the request line open. You may hear wedding bells on it but God don't ever play the blues.

Chapter 28

BLUE CHRISTMAS

One thing about small, rural towns is they really do up the holidays. Fort Bragg was no exception. On a cold December night you could feel Christmas in the brisk air. The lively streets were strung with sparkling tinsel and the shops were all lit up like Toyland with fancy colored lights and other festive decorations. Not even a greeting card could capture the spirit of Christmas like downtown Fort Bragg. There's nothing quite like peering through a frosted storefront window with painted candy canes, then setting your eyes upon a nativity resting gently atop a blanket of white winter snow. It warms your heart. You want to celebrate even if you don't believe in Jesus... or Santa Claus... or a virgin birth in a blizzard.

As festive as Fort Bragg was, my spirits could not be lifted. Christmas of '77 would prove to be a huge downer for me. Nothing was going well. I hated my job. The people I worked for hated me. Roxanne and I weren't getting along well either. As soon as school break came she got on a bus and headed straight back to L.A. I didn't have a car because Roxanne had totaled the Pinto. It would be my first Christmas away from family. I would spend this one all by my lonesome, just poor little me. I played *'Blue Christmas'* by Elvis about as often as Bill requested *'Wedding Bell Blues'*.

I didn't care that I had to work both my shift and Dave's on Christmas Eve and Christmas Day. Nor did I whine about not getting paid extra for it. It wasn't going to ruin any of my plans. It didn't matter where I was or what I was doing, I'd be alone regardless. So, why not spin records for twelve hours? I'd be sure to pack eggnog and fruitcake in my lunch pail. And before the night was over I'd resurrect Elvis from the dead with his melancholy Christmas song. It was a lonely holiday, the loneliest ever, just me and the four drab walls of a quiet broadcast booth. It felt like a Charlie Brown Christmas, like that scene when he opens up the mailbox only to discover there is nothing for him. "I already know nobody likes me," he laments, "Do we need a special holiday to emphasize it?" I had nobody, no presents, no cards, no stuffed turkey, not even a drop of razzleberry dressing. But I had Elvis... Elvis and '*Blue Christmas*'.

Of course I was miserable, I was always miserable. Why should Christmas be any different? It was just another day. The magic it once held had melted away like the last frost of winter. And when spring arrived, and the sun came out, and the birds were singing, I was still moping by an empty mailbox with a cold chill in my heart. I had tried all kinds of things to pull myself out of my perpetual slump. I even bought Norman Vincent Peale's, 'The Power of Positive Thinking'. It was a total bust. It didn't work for me whatsoever. My mind didn't have the power to be positively manipulated by all the cerebral gymnastics it promoted. Or, maybe I was supposed to get off the weed first, I dunno'. Whatever the case, I couldn't find any answers in a paperback. Yet I was willing to try one more self-help book. I can't even remember what it was called. I just remember the picture of some vivacious redhead with her testimonial on the back cover. Her whole life had been radically transformed by a lecithin milkshake. An entire paperback dedicated to a milkshake, can you imagine? This was the power of positive drinking - one story after the next on how this frothy beverage saved an attractive redhead from some kind of mental nosedive. I bought all the ingredients. I whipped this sucker up, pinched my nostrils and guzzled her down three times a day. Nothin'!

My crisis was still there in the morning. Perhaps it only worked for redheads.

If Christmas was a drag the day after was a total let down. I got fired. Charles Granite was already in the studio when I showed up for my shift. He told me he had no other choice but to let me go. "The truth is, Terry," Charles enlightened me. "This is a small town. People talk." I knew exactly where he was headed. I could see every word sharpening themselves like daggers on the tip of his forked tongue. "They know about you and that girl you're living with," he continued, "It's a bad reflection on the station." I had little to say. With a half smile I simply responded, "I understand. It's okay with me." Charles' eyebrows flew up like tiny seagulls. It was as if he expected me to be devastated. "Don't take this too well, Terry." he chuckled. Honestly, I was relieved. I fully expected this to happen, I just didn't know when. Though I wasn't upset about losing my position I was angry about the timing. I felt used. It just seemed cruel to work me double shifts on Christmas Eve and Christmas Day then fire me the next morning. *Humbug!* Time for another pity party...

I thought about all the people who had hurt me, burned me, abused me and used me over the years. They were all 'religious folk'. The Granites had religion. Though Jay was a pervert, he too had religion. The handcuff happy Tom Fifer had religion. Joe Kelp, who falsely accused and shunned me, had religion. Even my dad claimed to have had religion. Don't get me wrong, some religious folk are moral people. Sadly they think that all their morality will save them. Then there are religious folk who are very immoral. They suppose all their religion will save them. I don't know which is worse. All I knew was I didn't like religion either way you sliced it.

*　　*　　*　　*　　*

153

What ultimately cost me my job at KQLH was my reputation. I had a bad one and, for the most part, I earned it. It really didn't take much effort either. I guess that's one of the major differences between a good reputation and a bad one; the one you have to work at, the other you don't. I didn't care much about reputation before I was a Christian but I do now. It seems that the early church placed a lot of stock in reputation as well. You may recall that when the apostles sent out a search party to find seven men who would serve as the first deacons (See Acts 6), the top qualifying factor was that they had to be of good reputation. I find this pretty remarkable in light of the fact that these deacons were being recruited to wait on tables!

The search party was then told *how* to identify men of good reputation. Firstly, they would be full of the Spirit. That really narrows things down when you think about it. Had this committee been told to find seven people full of religion, who knows what kind of screwballs they would have wound up with? Religion is not always a plus when it comes to reputation. As a matter of fact, you can be religious and have a real rotten reputation. The religious leaders in Jesus' day didn't score too high in the reputation department. They had reputations as 'vipers', 'hypocrites' and 'whitewashed tombs'. I don't know if I'd be flattered with a reputation for being religious. Now, a Spirit filled person - that's a person with a reputation! He's as genuine on the inside as he is on the outside.

Wisdom was the other tell-tell sign this search party was told to look for. People of good reputation tend to be full of wisdom. Personally, I believe wisdom comes as part of the package when you're filled with the Spirit. Whenever you read about someone being filled with the Spirit in the Bible they generally had profound things to say. Furthermore, they always acted sensibly

154

and even heroically at times. Those who spoke foolishly and acted cowardly were typically those who boasted of their religion. They put a lot of stock in the flesh and vehemently denied the working of God's Spirit. Because they rejected the Spirit they lacked wisdom and because they lacked wisdom they lacked character. As a result their reputations suffered immensely. There is an undeniable tie between character and reputation. That's why we need the Holy Spirit, He shapes our character. And our character shapes our reputation.

Chapter 29

BROKEN HEARTS AND SHATTERED WINDOWS

I wasn't really sure why Roxanne went back to L.A. She claimed that she didn't want to spend Christmas in Fort Bragg but I think it had more to do with the tension between us. Things were real heated by this time. It also became obvious that Roxanne was seeking attention elsewhere. She did not hide the fact that she had developed a real fancy for Chris. For awhile there they were spending a lot of 'alone time' together in his trailer while I was at work. When I would return to get her, Chris would typically be wearing nothing but his gym shorts. That's what he generally wore while in the comfort of his own living room. He'd blast his heater and lounge around in faded, red gym shorts. That's all. And when Roxanne went over for visits she'd dress rather scantily herself. This went on for several weeks. I don't know if it was the weed or just the dynamic of our bizarre lifestyle but I never made an issue of it. It wasn't a big deal to me. Maybe Roxanne was hoping I'd get jealous but I never did. Then something happened between her and Chris. All of a sudden Roxanne wanted nothing more to do with the guy. It was as though he had broken her heart and she despised him for it. So I'm thinking she may have left for the holidays to get away from Chris as well. Maybe she just needed time to figure things out, I don't know. All I know is that she left.

Roxanne never actually said she was leaving permanently; it was my understanding this was nothing more than a temporary break. But since I had lost my job in Fort Bragg there was no real reason for her to return. Nor did it make sense for me to stay so I made arrangements to head back to L.A. as quickly as possible. I went out and (for $150) bought an old Buick to drive home in. This ugly heap was in sad shape, all banged up and rusty, but she ran fairly well during the initial test drive. I piled what little Roxanne and I owned in this dilapidated rattrap and headed for the highway. As it turned out, Ol' Betsy had a pretty serious radiator leak; I had to stop every couple miles or so to fill it. But after a long stretch of highway over the Bay Bridge in San Francisco the engine finally overheated and blew. The dead Buick ended up getting towed to a wrecking yard where it went home to be with the Lord. I rode out the last leg of my trip in a rented U-Haul truck. It's kind of silly when you think about it. Here I am in this huge cargo truck toting about eight boxes of worthless junk. Everything fit neatly into the cab next to me and the entire storage area in the back remained completely empty. Maybe I was an idiot at the time but it was the only option I could think of for one-way transportation.

I had only one place to go and that was home with my mom... my mom and Rick. In all fairness, things had greatly improved when I returned. The years had mellowed my brother and he wasn't swinging punches anymore. That aside, my homecoming was awkward at best. Even under the choicest of circumstances it is weird moving back in with your mother especially after claiming independence as a 'fully matured, wise, responsible, self reliant adult'. And there was no question in my mind that I was. It's just hard to convince others of that when you've got your mommy looking after you. I've always admired my mother but returning to the nest after flying free for so long just didn't set well with me. At twenty-one, I felt like a fish out of water flapping on the cold sand, waiting for the tide to roll in and sweep me back where I belonged. I needed to be in the deep and living with Mom just felt too shallow for me. After all I was man enough to maneuver a U-Haul.

Roxanne had also gone back to stay with her family. By this time evil Jay had taken up residence elsewhere so the coast was clear for her to return home. Before long we reconnected but it was very apparent that our connection was poor. She was already running with a new crowd, friends of her brother Jean, and she was feeling very single too. One of the guys, Andy, really had it bad for Roxanne. Even though he was already involved with another gal he was very upfront about his carnal desires even to the point of negotiating some kind of babe-trade with me. Roxanne was completely agreeable to his proposal and, surprisingly enough, so was Andy's girlfriend. But the whole idea made me sick to my stomach. I just wasn't the kind of guy who could wheel and deal with relationships, intimacy and emotions as if they were meaningless moves on a game board. That's the sensible part of me speaking and it's all true. Another factor was that Andy didn't have much to bargain with. His girlfriend was very homely looking and I think he was quite anxious to shake her off on someone else. But I wasn't going to be treated like his personal donation-station.

Regardless of what I thought about it Andy's indecent proposal opened my eyes to a hard reality. I had to face the facts about Roxanne. Her eagerness to be dealt like a trading card was my cue that our attachment was fizzling. Another tell-tell sign was we just didn't know how to get along anymore. The fact is things had always been rocky between us. Most the time we fought like cats and dogs; there would be hissing, scratching, slapping, pushing and hair pulling. By this stage in our relationship things had gotten extremely volatile. Generally after we'd get into it I would scream, "It's over, Roxanne, I'm breaking up with you!" Then I'd take my words back when our tempers died down. I'd break up with her a few times a week at least. Finally she got tired of me jerking her around. She warned me, "If you ever say 'it's over' again it will be the last time!" The next day we got into one of our usual knock-down-drag-out fights and I yelled, "It's over, Roxanne!" Her response was, "I warned you, Terry! That's it, it's over!" She held true to her word, we were finished. And Andy was waiting hungrily in the wings.

I was devastated by the break-up. We had spent over six years of our miserable lives together. She was my only girlfriend throughout high school and we shared a home for my entire three and a half years of cruddy adulthood. Interestingly enough, we never discussed things like marriage, or kids or one day growing old in a small wooden house with an herb garden. There was no discussion whatsoever about the future. We were just two confused souls caught in a common web of circumstance and tragedy. Roxanne was the girl who had to grow up quickly; I was the adult who refused to grow up at all. Though the break-up was inevitable it was painful nonetheless.

The thing that stinks about break-ups is the fear of the unknown. At least this was true for me. Roxanne was all I knew and that was enough to keep me hanging on for as long as I did. Breaking up only meant that the only continuity in my life since puberty would cease to be.

Even under the cruddiest circumstances relationships provide a security blanket. And when that comfortable woobie is yanked out from under your feet life feels very uncertain. I wondered if I'd ever love or be loved again and the greatest loss I grieved over was familiarity. When things screech to a sudden halt everything turns strange and scary, and there is no one next to you to hold your hand to guide you through it. Sadly though, when relationships are as unhealthy as ours was, the fear of the familiar can be an uglier monster to face than the fear of the unknown. I think that's what happened with Roxanne. That's why she checked out when she did. The familiar became very scary and the unfamiliar was looking more inviting all the time.

At only twenty-one years of age I felt my life was over. I had lost my live-in girlfriend, my job, my car and, when I moved back home I had lost my dignity along with everything else. The pain in my heart was unbearable, I cried desperately for days. Because my sorrows seemed so overwhelming, it was actually a good thing that I was home. Mom understood my suffering and became my only real source of comfort. However, in spite of all the love she offered I knew my stay would be brief. My belongings remained boxed up in the garage. And truthfully, I wasn't emotionally ready to deal with those boxes. Opening them would be like opening up the wounds of my heart. I just wasn't stable enough to go through the painful process of sorting my stuff from Roxanne's.

I should have gathered her belongings sooner but that task was a low priority in my state of utter destitution. But waiting didn't set well with Roxanne. One afternoon she came knocking at the door. Too upset to answer I just called out, "What do you want?" Her demand was simple, "I want my record albums!" I told her to come back after I had everything all sorted out but she was persistent and kept demanding, *"I want them now!"* I refused to give in to the little nag. *"Later!!!"* I fired back. Then Roxanne went as ballistic as our lumberjack neighbor in Fort Bragg. She started punching out the small decorative windows in the door with her fists! *"I want them now!"* she screamed, as shattered glass flew into the entryway. Roxanne punched her way through then helped herself to the locked door handle. After a hairy screaming match I opened the garage door and led her to the stack of boxes. "Dig in!" I growled. She tore through all the boxes until she found her albums. Then, with blood, cuts and scrapes on her fingers, she left with Stevie Wonder, Chaka Kahn and all her other musical friends.

I was still repairing the broken windows when my mother came home from work. "What on earth happened?" Mom asked with a shocked look on her face. "Roxanne was here." I sighed. Nothing more needed to be said.

Chapter 30

THE CON WHO CAME TO KESTER

Guy Hemp was a fellow I had known ever since the third grade. We went to elementary, junior high and high school together. Though we were well acquainted, Guy wasn't somebody I had ever wanted to hang out with. I always thought of him as a two-bit, smooth talkin' schemer. Even as a young child he came off that way. He wasn't one to make real friends but saw the people in his life as easy prey for his self-serving conquests. If a kid had money Guy would chum up to him. If a student was popular on campus Guy would follow in his shadow. And Guy loved the entertainment business, so if a fella' showed talent, he'd be puckering up to his backside. I never thought in my wildest imagination that I would ever be living with this scoundrel. But I did, dismissing his past behavior as the immature wiles of a pubescent juvenile. Yes, I had convinced myself that somehow manhood had changed him. I quickly learned that it changed him about as much as it had changed me.

In some respects Guy was different than he had been at school. Physically speaking, manhood had transformed this scrawny punk into a well chiseled hunk. He stood six-foot-six with the frame of a Spartan warrior. I, on the other hand, was tall, frail and lanky. I looked like a poster child for a concentration camp. Guy would strut around our apartment buck naked from time to time, just in case I should ever question his masculinity. I'd pretend not to notice. If he was trying to intimidate me it was overkill. I already had a huge inferiority complex without Guy's help. In a world of what I perceived to be 'real men' I often felt like Pinocchio. It seemed as if God had deprived me of those 'macho' characteristics that dreamers so desperately covet: chest hair, brawn, a deep voice, athletic ability and a knack for picking up girls. I was nothing but a beanpole with a baby face. Not even my moustache was entirely real. Without the aid of eyebrow pencil it wasn't much more than peach fuzz. Looking back, I think I was more like Pinocchio than I realized. I had a Jiminy Cricket by my side. Guy didn't. He had no conscience whatsoever. He used his all charm and other God given assets to prey upon others, especially women. I doubt they thought of Guy as a man after they got taken. With hindsight they may have actually preferred a beanpole with a conscience!

*　　*　　*　　*　　*

Slowly but surely I picked up the pieces of my life. I was trying to anyway. Before long I found myself back at *The Summerhouse* with charred tongs and a greasy spatula in my sweaty palms. It was a humbling experience to go from spinning records back to flipping grilled salmon but I did it. I bought a new car too. Well, it wasn't actually that new, it was a 1960 Rambler with a flathead six. This baby had a lot of character to it and she ran like a top. I actually fell in love with her. What can I say? After losing everything even a Rambler can steal your heart. Jobs are unreliable. Relationships also hold a degree of uncertainty. But one can always depend on a Rambler!

I was dining at a restaurant in Northridge when I ran into Guy. He was in the next booth. We both did double takes as we recognized each other. I hadn't seen Guy since high school. Boy, had he changed. He was a giant! His shoulders were as broad as he was tall and he spoke with a booming voice that would shake the ears off an elephant. This two-legged leviathan and I had found ourselves in a similar predicament. His wife had given him the boot and, like me, he needed a place to live. We each saw the answer to our dilemmas in one another. Within a week's time we were rooming together in a Van Nuys

164

apartment on Kester Avenue.

Guy worked part-time as a bouncer at a club called *The Rock Corporation*. To Guy, though, bouncing wasn't really work. It was more like recreation to him. He enjoyed a good brawl and coming home with a blood stained shirt was like placing a shiny new trophy on the mantle. It was another reminder that he was a true man, a big man, one not to be messed with. Other than bouncing for a few hours a week Guy didn't work much. He didn't need to. He made money scamming people. It always amazed me how folks could be so easily suckered by Guy. I could see his bluff coming a mile away. Maybe he just knew how to choose his victims. Or maybe it was because they didn't know Guy as well as I did. I suspect it was a little of both.

A regular feeding ground for Guy was the *94th Aero Squadron*, a popular discothèque located near the Van Nuys Airport, which we would often frequent together. I'd disappear beyond the starry lights of the disco ball while Guy roamed the floor. He'd sashay around with his flashy sports jacket with big lapels all the while eyeballing the crowd, formulating his hit list. Without fail, there was always some sorry damsel longing to be found in his handsome company. They'd drink, they'd dance, and they'd flirt and have a fling. The next thing she knew, she was out some cash. These gals became so infatuated with Guy they'd just hand him the money. He'd tell them he was a budding television star in a yet-to-be released sitcom. "The check is in the mail!" Guy would say. "A big fat one!" But he always needed some quick funds to carry him over, a few C notes was all, just until he could cash that humongous check he was expecting. Usually the ladies bought into his spiel. He didn't always clean up in the hundreds but he generally came out pretty good. And before long some angry father would be pounding on our door. Guy would flash me the signal not to answer. I never did.

I wasn't any saint but I didn't care for Guy's antics, especially when he started preying upon our kindly neighbors. We had a recreation room at our apartment complex and from time to time Guy and I would hang out there and play some pool. When it came to billiards, the big fella' had game. He'd smoke me every time. Not that that was any great feat but it was more than obvious that he was a sharp shooter. But he would pretend to be less than average with our trusting neighbors. So naturally, when he challenged them to a contest with bets on the table they readily accepted. There was one match where I attempted to tip off the unsuspecting victim but Guy turned around and belted me in the mouth. After one bloody lip I never joined him in the rec room again.

Kip and his mom, Sally, also got taken by Guy. They lived immediately next door to us. When Kip needed a car Guy made him an offer he couldn't refuse. He proposed to sell him his late 60's model MG convertible. This baby was in perfect mint condition and turned a lot of heads on the road. When Guy agreed to sell it for half the blue book value Kip jumped at the opportunity. The only snag was Guy needed to hang onto the vehicle for another week or so. But he was willing to secure the special purchase price for an earnest deposit of $500 which Kip gladly paid, with a little help from his poor mother. Within a few short days Guy quickly had a change of heart about selling his MG. It was also about this time that the earnest money couldn't be accounted for.

With all the people Guy was ripping off I sensed my safety was in jeopardy. It would only be a matter of time before I was caught in the crossfire of a heartless huckster and some sorry sucker. My goal was to be out before the fecal material hit the rotary blades of the cooling device. Though I knew I had to bail

166

out quickly I also realized it couldn't be while Guy was around. I'd be a fool to even make mention of my intentions. He'd just rip me off of what little I had. I had discovered that he was already stealing from me. The cash I was hiding in my Chinese puzzle box was mysteriously disappearing. When I'd confront Guy about it he'd just play stupid and say, "I don't even know how to open that thing!"

My big moment came when Guy was admitted to the hospital for appendicitis. I would never wish appendicitis on anyone but I was truly grateful for the window of escape provided for me when Guy got it. In those few short days he was laid up next to a bed pan I gathered all my belongings and vanished into the night. That was the last I ever saw of the con who came to Kester.

Chapter 31

YOU SCHMOOZE, YOU LOSE

If there was one thing Guy knew how to do well it was to schmooze. He was charming, polite and always practiced proper etiquette. His smile was as infectious as love in the springtime and his handshake was firm. He was a man who honored the rules of chivalry. He opened doors for the ladies and offered his seat to the elderly. Though he didn't smoke himself he always carried a cigarette lighter as a courtesy for those who did. To the unsuspecting he was a dream. Those who to his lure soon found that Guy was a nightmare. Behind the sweet smoke and flattering mirrors lurked an evil predator. Sure he was a gentleman who would offer his seat to a senior. But he was also listening for a jingle in the old man's pocket as he lowered himself. Certainly, he would hold the door for a lady... all the while checking for a brand label on her backside. That's how Guy operated. That's how he paid the rent. He was a con.

Guy was slick and grew increasingly more confident by the day. He had convinced himself that he could talk anyone into or out of anything and I must admit that he was quite successful - most of the time... but not all of the time. There were those rare occasions when charm would disappoint and finesse would leave Guy out in the cold. Such a time was when he attempted to make an appearance at the Academy Award Ceremony in Tinsel Town.

Oscar Night. It would be the ultimate date with the girl he so desperately longed to impress. Sure she would go with him. After all Guy was an actor, though not the kind she was led to believe. Barbara was flattered by the invitation. She got dolled up in her flashiest evening gown. Guy wore that familiar suit with giant lapels and dowsed himself with the sweetest fragrance Thrifty Drugstore had to offer. Then off the darling couple went. Can't you just picture the two of them zooming away together in his shiny red convertible MG? So can I. But that's not how it went down. His car wouldn't start so... they took mine... without permission, by the way. Now can you picture them? Can you see them rolling up alongside the Limos and Bentleys in my oxidized white 1960 Rambler? Can you see these crazy characters cranking down the window to wave at Jack Nicholson?

I don't know how far away they had to park. I don't know how close to the red carpet they came. What I do know is this, Guy and his lovely date weren't admitted to the Academy Award ceremonies. All the charm in the world could not open doors for these two to join the glitz of Hollywood's most celebrated event. Finesse could not get them seated among the rich and famous. Sometimes you win and sometimes you schmooze. But on Oscar night, schmoozers are losers. There is only one way to get on the red carpet, your name must be recorded on the guest list. Unfortunately, Guy's wasn't. Neither was Barbara's. That was that.

The Kingdom of God operates in a similar fashion. You can't schmooze your way in. It won't matter how polite you come across or how fancy you are dressed. Nor will it matter what you are driving or how close to the red carpet you may be. Unless your name is on the guest list you won't make it in. These aren't my rules; they come straight from the Word of God. With regard to that heavenly paradise scripture states, *"Nothing unclean, no one who does anything detestable, and no liars will ever enter it. Only those whose names are written in the lamb's Book of Life will enter it."* (See Revelation 21:27) The obvious

170

question at this point is: how does one get their name in the Book of Life?

      *   *   *   *   *

This might come as a shocker but many religious leaders do not have their names written in the Book of Life. Hard to believe, I know, but it's true. And if that weren't shocking enough, there are oodles of unsavory sorts who somehow get their names inked in on God's guest list. Doesn't sound fair, does it? The reality is, if we were able to flip trough it's many pages we would discover a host of unlikely candidates listed. Honestly, we're talkin' real questionable characters here. A rap sheet on just one of these low-lifer's would be enough to Paper Mache' the entire planet! One might even be tempted to tip God off on offenses He seemingly overlooked on some of these rascals. (Before you get any ideas, though, you may want to check out your own rap sheet.)

Jesus informed the religious leaders of His day that they weren't on the guest list but that hookers and swindlers were. (See Matthew 21:31) He didn't actually use the terms 'hookers' or 'swindlers' but that's how we might express it today. Jesus actually referred to these creatures as harlots and tax collectors. In New Testament times you couldn't stoop much lower than to be a hooker or a tax collector, they were bottom of the barrel. Both were predators, neither had an ounce of dignity. Tax collectors took cash against a person's will while harlots took it against one's better judgment. One stole money for pleasure while the other sold pleasure for money. They enriched their livelihoods at the expense of others. One forced while the other flirted but the end result was always the same, somebody got taken. That is why, at least in Jesus' day, they earned the scorn of all society.

171

How could it be that God would prefer tramps and thieves over such noble gents as priests, scribes and temple elders? Scarier yet, does He still operate this way today? Who is on the guest list? Is it the good reverend with the white collar? Or, Bambi the streetwalker who won't even button her collar? Who will it be; the priest who prays at the parish? Or, the bamboozler who preys at the pool hall? Hold on... wait a minute... what was that verse again? *"Nothing unclean, no one who does anything detestable, and no liars will ever enter it. Only those whose names are written in the lamb's Book of Life will enter it."* Now, let's make some sense of this. Aren't harlots unclean? Is not the work of a crook detestable? Yes and yes! One lies in the sack while the other lies through his teeth! We appear to have stumbled upon a gross contradiction here. Jesus unlocks that mystery in the following parable:

"What do you think about this? A man had two sons. He went to the first and said, 'Son, go to work in the vineyard today.' His son replied, 'I don't want to!' But later he changed his mind and went. The father went to the other son and told him the same thing. He replied, 'I will, sir,' but he didn't go. Which of the two sons did what the father wanted?" "The first," they answered. Jesus said to them, "I can guarantee this truth: Tax collectors and prostitutes are going into the kingdom of God ahead of you." - Matthew 21:28-30

This second son sure was an agreeable young sort, wasn't he? He definitely could talk the talk. But like my friend Guy, he was nothing but a schmoozer. When it was time for the rubber to meet the road he back peddled all the way. It was the first son that ultimately threw himself in gear by submitting to his father's will. Yet, it took a change of heart to move him in the right direction.

Two sons. Two pictures. With the first son we see a marvelous picture of repentance which is evidenced by a change of heart. He regrets the poor choice he initially made and goes to the vineyard where he reaps fruits of righteousness. Not so with son number two. He is an example of the unregenerate life. Pleasing the father is low on his list. This fellow is nothing but a yes-man. Though the intention may initially be there, the follow through is not. He's more interested in doing his own thing and avoids the vineyard without any regret whatsoever. He, too, will reap what he has sown.

Two sons, two kinds of people. Those who do and those who don't. The repentant and unrepentant. However you slice it there are just two kinds of people. Those who have their names recorded in the Book of Life and those who do not. In the big scheme of things it comes down to this: you schmooze, you lose. No one gets on the guest list by being a yes-man. A yes-man says 'yes' on Sunday but his actions dictate otherwise on Monday. He prays like an angel but plays like the devil. He's got enough religion to make him look alive on the outside but he's dead on the inside. You'll find his name on the church roster but not in the Book of Life.

The Kingdom of God is reserved for those who've had a true change of heart. With a change of heart the doors of heaven open wide for the harlot, the crook, the adulterer and the drunk. Without a change of heart neither the pastor, preacher nor Sunday school teacher makes it through the pearly gates. That's just the way it is. There must first be brokenness. There must be repentance, a turning from 'my will' to 'thy will'. Then and only then do our names appear in the Book of Life. You see, it's a family album. You must become a child of God. We do that by surrendering to the Father and accepting His only begotten Son,

173

Jesus Christ as Lord and Savior. Once we do that we are given a new heart and that's when the heavenly Bic® goes *click*. Then our name is written where no eraser can ever remove it. The only thing that gets erased is our sin.

*   *   *   *   *

Like Oscar night there is a huge award ceremony in heaven. The major difference is that everyone on God's guest list is a winner and we all receive handsome awards. Another distinction would be that the Academy generally invites an elite group of actors. Chances are you've been excluded. I know I have. But God's invitation goes out to everyday people. Not those who put on a great performance but sincere people who are ready to get real with the Lord. If that's your desire He's eager to roll out the red carpet for you.

Chapter 32

HELLO DARKNESS MY OLD FRIEND

Dark. That is the only way to describe the house I moved into after checking out on Guy. It was dark and smoky. Other than that it was just your typical tract home in the suburbs of L.A. It wasn't typically cared for though. No one cleaned, no one mowed. No one really did much of anything. We just sat around with blank looks on our faces, vegetating on thrashed sofas as we stared at the nasty grime on the pale walls. There were four bedrooms and four of us who paid for them. By day we worked, by night we sat... in the smoke... heady smoke exhaled from our lungs out into the dark atmosphere of our dismal lair.

Meet Paul. He's the one who leased the property and rented rooms to the rest of us. I liked Paul, we got along well. He sold weed but it was free to those who paid him rent money. I never got this perk anywhere else so I considered Paul to be a very benevolent landlord. Then there was Richard. He and Paul had gone to school together and were old friends. Richard also took advantage of the freebies that came with renting a room but he liked to drink as well. Actually, we all enjoyed a cold beer now and then. But Richard drank more frequently than that. Make that a lot more frequently. Truthfully, I don't ever remember seeing him sober. He'd generally get bombed and pass out in the same beat-up, old chair. He was a pleasant fellow, though. You couldn't help but love the guy. Like Otis, the town drunk on Mayberry RFD, Richard was a likable character. Finally, there was Dave. He's the one who ate lamb with me at Gordo's. Dave and I saw a lot of each other. We worked together, lived together and got stoned together. The two of us got along just fine. All four of us did. It was a peaceful house; peaceful, dark and smoky.

I learned very quickly that whatever was brought into the house was to be "shared". I learned this sore lesson the first time I bought groceries. I purchased a whole week's worth, a whole week's worth intended for me alone. The refrigerator and pantry had been completely bare before I stacked all my yummy consumables upon the empty shelves. They were just as bare the following day - after a feeding frenzy which, sad to say, I was never invited to. I never went grocery shopping again after that. I ate out. We all did. We would have to had been stupid not to. Sharing weed is one thing, supplying potheads who suffer from an acute case of 'chronic munchie syndrome' is quite another. My budget didn't allow for it. The three hungry piranhas would have to get their Twinkies elsewhere.

Because Paul was a dealer there was a constant flow of people coming through our doors. Many who bought weed were acquaintances of Paul so they hung around and chatted while sampling the goods. Often I'd find myself sitting in our dark, smoke filled living room engaging with people I didn't even know. Some folks get real talkative when they're high. Others, like me, become completely withdrawn. I'd get this big stupid grin on my face which I couldn't control if my life depended on it. It made me self conscious to the point of paranoia. Worse yet, I'd always get stuck next to one of the talkative stoners. I'd be gawking at him with my glazed face and dopey smile, all the while hoping he wouldn't notice how utterly ridiculous I looked. To add to my fears, I never understood one word of anything said to me when I was high. I knew I'd be doomed if ever solicited for any kind of feedback.

So, why did I do it? Why, oh, why did I get high? I suppose for the same reason the proverbial chicken crossed the road, to get to the other side! There is that fleeting moment between the urge to get high and lighting up when you realize that truth is a whole lot scarier than the imagined. Deep down I understood that the fears I had while stoned were totally irrational. They were nothing more than inventions of an altered mind. On the other hand, the things I was escaping from were very real. I had been abandoned by people I loved, accused by people I looked up to and abused by people I trusted. So, pot became a cozy, warm blanket that covered all my pain, hurt and anger. When I wrapped myself in it, I was all grins. For these reasons I liked smoking pot. I know that's a little shocking to hear from a man of God but it's true; I liked it. Besides, paranoia only struck when I had to deal with people I didn't know. In my own comfort zone, though, I didn't fight the dopey grin. Actually, it felt good to smile so much. But when reality raised its ugly head the smile abandoned me. Betrayed by my own stupid smirk! I knew only one way to get it back but I didn't know how to keep it.

Pot was the only thing the four of us had in common besides music. We loved the same kind of music, the Rock n' Roll blues. We loved all the same artists: Eric Clapton, Steve Winwood, Eric Clapton, Dave Mason, Eric Clapton, Joe Walsh and Eric Clapton. If you ever want to know about a rock artist the person to ask is a stoner. People think I know a lot about music because I spent a few years in radio. This is true. But a lot of that knowledge also comes from sitting around and getting high. Pretty much, that's all potheads do, listen to music. As for me and my roommates, the only literature we ever read was album covers and record sleeves. We familiarized ourselves with the producers, the players, the songwriters and the people they gave thanks to. If you were to ask any of us what was going on in

177

the world socially, economically or politically we wouldn't have had a clue. But we could tell you in an instant who played with Eric Clapton on the song '*Layla*'!

Life grew drearier with each new day in the dark house. Our misery was our only company. Darkness hid the ugly truth of our horrid surroundings: pale walls, filthy floors, tattered sofas and fallen countenances in search of a grin. We were lost. The light switches remained in the off position. The only glow to be found was at the end of a joint, which we passed from one desperate face to the next.

*   *   *   *   *

Frankly, I don't understand why a Christian would choose to get high but I honestly understand why an unbeliever would. In the realm of unbelief reality isn't all that pleasant. The real world offers few answers and little hope for the abandoned, abused and brokenhearted. Then there are the uncertainties surrounding an unbeliever's eternal future. With regard to these issues, the best our world can offer is a cozy little blanket wrapped in a Zig-Zag. Things are not so bleak for the Christian, though. In fact, we enter into a whole new reality, one we long to run to and not from. In Christ Jesus we find healing from our hurts and hope for our future. These things are best enjoyed in a right state of mind and with a heart that has been altered by His amazing touch.

Chapter 33

A JEW CAME THROUGH
Or was it Two?

In vivid contrast there was Jeff... a young, Jewish busboy who worked with me at The Summerhouse. Whenever I saw him he was talking up Jesus. Below is a brief bio of Jeff from the website of *Bear Valley Church* where he (at the time of this writing) serves as senior pastor.

> *Dr. Jeff Kaplan was born on February 3, 1960 in Los Angeles to Marcy and Jordan Kaplan. As one might guess by his last name, Jeff was born and raised Jewish. He had a traditional Bar Mitzvah and grew up celebrating the four major Jewish high holidays with his family. During his high school years, Jeff recognized that there was something missing in his life. At the age of eighteen, Jeff chose to attend a mass at a Catholic church for the first time. Even though no one had shared the gospel with Jeff, the Lord spoke to his heart. As a result, Jeff embraced Jesus into his life as his personal Savior and Lord.* [15]

Jeff was just a pup when we met. He was eighteen; I was a mature twenty-two. At least I thought I was. I got to know Jeff shortly after his Catholic mass experience, the one that ultimately brought him to his knees. He was no longer attending mass when we became friends but was exploring churches of the more protestant persuasion. Though he was still trying to find his place in Christendom one thing was clear, Jeff had a passion for Jesus. Perhaps that was what appealed to me most about

---

[15] www.bearvalleychurch.org

him. He wasn't pimping a particular church or some denomination; he was simply proclaiming his Lord and Savior. Nevertheless, I wasn't an easy nut to crack.

Jeff clung to my side like a barnacle, sharing the gospel whenever he could. It wasn't just with me; Jeff was telling everybody about his newfound faith in Jesus Christ. I knew where he was coming from, though. I'd been there and heard it all before. With my Catholic upbringing and brief stint as a born-again Baptist, my insights into Christianity gave me a much greater edge over my fanatical friend. Our exchanges became a match of wits. *Who was the more enlightened one, he or I?* By this time my belief system had become very convoluted. It wasn't that I was making an attempt to grasp higher truth; it was more like I preferred an adulterated version of it. After all, subjective truth presents some convenient loopholes which aren't available in a world of absolutes. So long as you're in the ballpark subjectivity will say you're okay. But if you're hung up on absolutes the only way to score a run is to focus on home plate. That's a little narrow for some. As for me, I was in the ballpark somewhere out in left field. I had come to a place where I reasoned that all religions had merit. Each had something sweet to say about God and all taught the wonderful virtues of leading a good life. (And, certainly, that's what I was all about!) But, what made Christianity so special? As long as I could plead ignorance on that one point I could justify my pathetic lifestyle.

Almost every day Jeff and I would enter into a genial sparring match as we discussed his 'narrow belief' that Jesus was the only way to home plate. I met every argument he had with ridicule and sarcasm. He preached while I patronized. As he testified I teased. Jeff used his mind while I used my mouth. That's what I typically resorted to when backed into a corner. It was the only defense I had. And it worked about as well with Jeff as it did with the gang bangers at Lanark Park. He still came out swinging. Don't get me wrong, Jeff and I weren't enemies by any stretch. Ours was your basic friendly fire of testosterone between two males bonding. The very thing we differed upon is what brought us together as dear ol' chums.

I never really gave much thought to the things Jeff told me about Jesus, not consciously anyway. Most of the time, I'd just laugh him off. Then I'd go home to my dark and dreary house, get high and listen to the Rock n' Roll blues with Paul, Richard and Dave. As odd as it may sound, I felt safe in the darkness. All the putrid smoke seemed to camouflage my hurt and shame. And that familiar dopey grin made me believe, at least for a moment, that I was verging upon a state called happiness. This path to Utopia normally took a detour to the donut shop then brought me back home in a sugar coma. It was a pitiful existence, one which subjective truth can't save a person from. That's because you're in your own ballpark. You decide what is foul and what isn't. No one ever strikes out and everyone walks. And the referees are all out in left field telling you you're safe.

I'm certain Jeff must have felt at times that he was casting pearls before swine with me. Not even I realized his message was getting through. It would be a gross exaggeration to say I was seeking God in this season of my life. I wasn't. I was seeking only to escape. But then light broke through that cozy blanket I was hiding under. Honestly, I was high as a kite when it happened. As per usual, we were all smoking grass in our dark living room. I remember things getting really quiet in my mind. Unlike the Apostle Paul's Damascus road experience when he heard a loud voice, I heard stillness. It was like a light switch came on and all of a sudden I wasn't high anymore. Then I began to think about Jeff and how his life was so much different than mine. He had joy and I was miserable. His life had purpose, mine was a waste. He had peace and my life was a mess. The only thing I could attribute these things to was - he had Jesus and I didn't.

Quietly I excused myself to my room. There I sat upon the very bed that knew my sorrows more than any mortal being and I thought about how pitiful my life was. My fingers fumbled for the nightstand and latched upon the dusty Bible my sister, Kathy, gave me on my fifteenth birthday. Truthfully, I had never read it before, other than looking up an occasional verse back when I still made appearances at the Baptist church. Though those days were long gone I had held onto the Holy Book for sentimental reasons. But something caused me to explore the scriptures that evening. I didn't know exactly where to turn so I just pinched a chunk of pages and randomly flipped the Book open. Then a verse from Matthew jumped right out and clobbered me over the noggin. The passage I landed on was this:

"Thou shalt love the Lord thy God with all thy heart, and with all thy soul, and with all thy mind."
Matthew 22:37 (KJV)

If I have ever felt like a sinner it was then. I was convicted by the mother of all commandments, the one which Jesus qualified as the absolute greatest. It nailed me. The blame game ended, the victim card got trumped and any lingering notions of me being a good person quickly diminished. I was without excuse. With all my other many sins it seemed I could point the finger elsewhere: this person, that person, environment or genetics. But nothing got me off the hook when it came to the great commandment. The ugly truth was I didn't love God. And there was no one to blame but me. Confronted by the pure and absolute Word of God I broke down in tears and with a broken and contrite heart

I pleaded for forgiveness. It was not the formulated sinner's prayer I repeated on Van Nuys Boulevard with Stan Angel. This time I was desperate; I wanted sin out and Jesus in.

God heard my cry and moved in a powerful and miraculous way; one which eternity will never erase from my memory. There in the still of my bedroom the Spirit of the Lord fell upon me and I sensed total forgiveness. All the guilt of everything I had ever done was instantly lifted. Furthermore, all the shame, anger and hurt I carried as a result of those who sinned against me was completely removed. I know this isn't everybody's experience when they are born again but it was mine, I was totally healed of all my sorrow and pain. God removed my misery and filled me with peace, hope and joy. Being washed of the Spirit I fell to my knees as tears of sorrow turned to tears of joy. We'll leave it for the theologians to debate whether or not I was truly saved at fourteen. What I do know for certain is that for the first time in my life I finally had the assurance of salvation. I have not questioned it since. My life was forevermore changed.

I couldn't wait to announce the news to Jeff that Jesus was now in my heart. When I told him at work the next day he didn't take me seriously. He was waiting for the punch line, quite convinced I was subjecting him to more of my vicious ridicule. Maybe he was even a little doubtful that the Lord could use a kid like him to reach someone as lost as me. Whatever the case, Jeff soon realized I wasn't joking around and that the Lord had worked through him to open my eyes. And it was Jeff who took me under his wing and helped establish me in my new Christian walk.

Chapter 34

PRETZEL MAN

It had been years since I stepped foot into a church. After all my bad experiences at First Baptist I had thrown in the towel on organized religion altogether. Frankly speaking, I suffered no great loss when I kissed religion goodbye. *Good riddance!* I have since learned that Jesus had His own issues with a super-structure religious system. Furthermore, many of the epistles speak against churches with human hands working fervently at the crank. However, I went over the edge in my thinking. Neither Jesus nor the authors of the various epistles ever copped an attitude toward the church. Their desire was to see this divine institution freed from all the putrid religious rigmarole that gave it such a foul stench. That was not my heart at all. I lumped religion and church in the same waste basket and threw the baby out with the bath water. This left me a little apprehensive about getting back into fellowship. But I was willing to give it another shot. I agreed to go to church with Jeff on the very Wednesday after I gave my heart to Christ. There were actually a couple of us that were invited. Brett, another co-worker of ours, also came along. Jeff had been sharing the gospel with him as well. Like me, Brett had walked with Jesus at one time but fell back into the world's relentless grip. Unlike me, though, he had not yet come to his senses. But by the grace of God we all went together, the zealot, the heathen and me, the repentant sinner, to a church neither of us had ever before attended.

The fellowship was called 'Rancho por Dios' and its members met in a small rented chapel behind a large church building in Chatsworth on Topanga Canyon Boulevard. Pastor Sam worked full time as a successful building contractor. Before giving his life to Christ he was a terrible alcoholic and would beat his wife.

After the Lord delivered him he wanted to help others with addictions. He led many to the Lord, opened his home and helped rehabilitate these young people by giving them work in construction. What began as Bible studies for drug addicts in Sam's living room soon evolved into a small, independent church in Chatsworth. And, according to what Jeff was told, when Sam spoke it was like hearing the voice of God.

Other than a mysterious 'voice of God' we really didn't know what to expect when we found ourselves in front of the large double doors. Nervously we snuck in and sat toward the back so as not to disturb the worship service which was already in progress. On the small stage stood a cluster of freaky folks who looked more like my roommates than they did music ministers. This team did not resemble the choir I had grown familiar with at First Baptist. They had guitars and drums and one even had a banjo. I was accustomed to this style of worship when I attended the Mustard Seed but never had imagined I'd ever hear it in a holy sanctuary. Some might say the church had sold out by embracing a modern style of music. Others would argue they were simply getting back to their early roots. All I really knew was it introduced me to a form of worship which I found heartfelt, and a path to God's presence that old red hardbacks can't always deliver in a contemporary world.

I also found the congregation quite intriguing. It wasn't a large group, only about sixty in all. As I looked around to survey the modest sized assembly I instantly noticed something quite unusual. I fit in! These were folks I could easily identify with. They were everyday people just like me. No one was there dressed to impress, everyone was casual. Simply put, they were themselves. It was a place where one could feel comfortable just being what God made him to be without ever having to feel judged. Obviously I do not know the heart of man as God does but from everything I could observe these were real people. They all had genuine expressions of joy on their faces.

Of all the people in the small chapel there was one fellow who caught my eye more than any other. He sat in a wheelchair. His crumpled body was so frail he lacked the strength to hold his head in an upright position; it just hung over to the side. His thin, crooked arms twisted like a pretzel across his twig frame as his scrawny legs dangled beneath him. What drew my attention to this young gentleman more than his physical impairments was the peaceful countenance on his concave face. He seemed to be more content in his feeble state than I had ever been in mine. Somewhere deep inside that skeletal figure was a giant who had discovered joy's secret.

After the hairy band of musical misfits disappeared from the stage a silver haired saint stepped up to the pulpit and introduced himself as Sam. Not reverend, not father, not pastor, just plain ol' Sam. Instantly I was on a first name basis with a preacher who preferred to talk to the flock rather than at them. This was something I had never before experienced in the church and, personally, I found it quite refreshing. Sam was hitting near sixty but was rugged and sturdy like a mountain. He had big, strong hands and a leathery face which bore testimony to his many years as a builder. And the rumor proved true. When he spoke it was exactly how you would imagine God to sound. His voice resonated with conviction and authority.

I don't recall what Sam shared that Wednesday evening, only that the three of us who came together were riveted to the pew. At the end of his message Sam invited anyone who needed prayer to come forward to the altar. Without any hesitation Brett responded to the invitation and stood fast to his feet. Ready to surrender his life back to Jesus he proceeded up the isle. Soon I saw others rise up. And in the midst of the flow was the pretzel man using every ounce of strength he could muster to wheel himself to the altar. My heart sank as I watched him. His prospects did not look good. I could easily predict the outcome of this hopeless endeavor. Pretzel man would coast up to the altar... hands would be laid upon him followed by vociferous demands for divine healing then... nothing. He'd roll back to his pew in the same sad shape, with hopes dashed for the billionth time. I'd seen it before. But... that's not what happened.

The pretzel man had no intentions of praying for himself. He slowly rolled up next to Brett, placed his scrawny arm upon his shoulder then gently whispered, "How can I pray for you?" And there at that humble altar the little giant in the wheel chair led Brett into a prayer of rededication. This offered me a picture of Christian love that left me absolutely breathless. It blew me away that the one person who appeared to be in need of the most prayer would set aside his own wants to lift up someone else. Right then the Lord spoke to my heart and said, "Forget about all your wretched experiences with organized religion, this is what true Christianity is!" Even to this day I look back to the pretzel man as my shining example of what real ministry is all about.

Once the service finally ended, my friends and I found ourselves quickly surrounded by the entire congregation. Not in an overwhelming way but in a most welcoming way. The people were so warm and so eager to embrace us into their loving family. The interest they showed in us was unmistakably genuine. They offered me something I was never able to find in the outside world, something my heart truly longed for. It's that wonderful little thing called acceptance. For me that meant I would be safe with these people. There was no threat of ever being looked down upon or judged. There would be no false accusations or anyone saying, "Yer kind ain't welcome 'round here." This was a place where I could settle in quite comfortably. It was a community I could enjoy being part of. It was a body that had a place for me. *Rancho por Dios* ultimately became my new church home. I would know the preacher as Sam and the pretzel man as John, and they would be my brothers. It wasn't the church for Jeff or for Brett but the small fellowship of misfits in the rented chapel became my new family.

Chapter 35

MOVING ON

In this drama we call 'being' there are two authors. There is us and there is the Author of life. When we hand the pen over to God He does not pick up where we leave off. He does not close one chapter then open another. He rewrites the entire story. This is something He must do as the story we write has a very tragic ending. The main character dies leaving no chance for a sequel. The story God writes has no ending at all, it moves like poetry from glory to glory. As an author I literally wrote one hell of a plot for myself. But now the narrative has changed. All the mistakes have been erased. The conflict has been resolved. The drama has ended and a new romance has begun. New characters have been introduced while old ones have been completely written out for good. This is needful, otherwise it's just the same old story.

*   *   *   *   *

I made some fast friends at *Rancho por Dios*, positive people who influenced me in the right direction. While my heart was drawn to seek more Christian fellowship old comfort zones began to feel extremely awkward. One of the places I no longer fit in was the house where I was living. It was as though the Light had broken through and I was finally able to see all the darkness of my dismal surroundings. If I was truly serious about making radical changes in my life I had no other option but to leave. I knew myself too well. I must be completely honest here; my decision to leave was not because I lost interest in smoking pot. On the contrary, I couldn't resist its sweet smell. Though God had freed me of all my guilt and shame, and though he had healed me of my many sorrows, His work wasn't quite finished.

The desire to get high still lurked within me. And that is why I knew I had to get out of temptation's way as soon as possible. It is important that we come to terms with our weaknesses. If it's sweets, don't hang out at the candy shop. It's that simple. Joseph did the right thing when he fled from Potiphar's wife. But we are kidding ourselves if we think he ran because he wasn't attracted to women. Is it possible he knew himself too well?

I wish I was one of those who could testify, 'I gave my heart to Christ and never got stoned again.' Bravo to those who can boast in such miracles but that's not my story. I fouled more than a few times. Not that I ever went looking for the stuff but when it was offered I was too weak to say no. It would be a stretch to say I was an addict but, the truth is, I did enjoy getting high. That's the reason why anyone sins; it is a hell of a lot of fun. And I mean that in the most literal sense. Hell offers a lot of jolly stops along the way so you can have a damned good time before you get there. Pardon the salty expletives but they do speak an unembellished truth. That said, the flop house I was living in offered too much opportunity for failure and I didn't want to blow things. It was time to move on.

After I returned to Southern California I had remained in touch with Chris in Fort Bragg. By divine coincidence (if you'll pardon the oxymoron) he was planning to move back to the L.A. area. Oddly enough, the Lord had also gotten hold of Chris through a high school buddy and he was interested in making changes in his life as well. Besides adjustments in his spiritual life Chris was also looking for a career change and wanted to pursue acting. With Hollywood calling his name Chris was ready to hang up the microphone at KDAC and head back south almost immediately. Not many days after our telephone chat we found ourselves combing Canoga Park together looking for an apartment. The next thing I knew, Chris and I were signing a rental agreement for a two bedroom apartment on Topanga Canyon Boulevard, not too far from *Rancho por Dios.* Paul was very understanding when I told him I'd be moving out on such short notice, but then most stoners tend to be very accommodating people. When you smoke pot you don't care much about anything. It's the ultimate apathy drug. Perhaps that's the scariest thing about it, you just quit caring about what's important and develop a lackadaisical attitude. Goals and aspirations lay dormant and you're not really concerned about how your life affects those around you or vice-versa. On the upside, it mellows you so you're not freaking out about things most folks tend to get uptight about. For example, when I was on pot I didn't stress out about my financial obligations. The fact is I didn't even give a rip. I'd throw my bills in the waste basket as quick as they came. So, even though you're not stressing out about things they do pile up and one day you have to face an ugly giant. I was finally ready to face mine, with the help of God, but I couldn't do it in a house full of potheads. So I packed what few things I owned and moved in with my old deejay buddy, Chris, into an environment that was completely drug and alcohol free.

My social life was definitely changing for the better. Mostly I'd spend time with Chris or Jeff, and sometimes all three of us would hang together. We had great times encouraging one another in the Lord but none of us attended the same church. Chris would go with his buddies to hear the charismatic preacher Jack Hayford at *The Church on the Way* while Jeff seemed to favor the more formal style of John McArthur at *Grace Community.* As for me, I avoided the mega-church madness and hung with the small cluster of misfits at *Rancho por Dios.* Even though I didn't have anyone to go with me I'd cruise to the small chapel in my old Rambler every Sunday morning and Wednesday night.

I became quite the social butterfly at the apartment complex too. Normally I'd lounge by the pool area where everyone else seemed to gather about. There I met a host of friendly neighbors, many of which were much older and retired. For some odd reason I seemed to connect with them more than anyone else. I suspect I felt safer with the elderly as most of the younger crowd in our complex appeared to be heavy partiers. Whatever the case was, I truly grew endeared to the older folks and they seemed to take a liking to me. Each day I'd sit out by the pool and engage in a game called Rook and listen to my gray haired friends reminisce about their younger years. The fact that I was no longer huddled among peers in a thick blur of smoke and spending time playing cards with senior citizens was evidence enough that God was doing some radical changes in me. For one thing He was teaching me how to love. I used to think love had a parasitical nature. Once bitten by it you became a constant drain, sucking everyone in your life dry. In other words, there was that desperate hunger for love but you're so focused on your own appetite it's never reciprocated. But now Jesus was opening wide the flow control of my heart. I could actually love people. I could love old people with a hand-sized deck of waxy cards. Or I could just sit with them and listen to their story just as you are listening to mine.

This love thing was turning out to be pretty cool. For the first time ever I found myself enjoying life where before I had been painfully trying to get through it. God had pulled me out from the wreckage and set me on a bright, new path. With my slate now clean I was ready to make responsible choices for myself. I found the words of Jesus to be true, that if you seek first the Kingdom of God and his righteousness, everything else just falls into place. (See Matthew 6:33) All I was really focusing on at the time was getting my spiritual life in order. That became my number one priority. Female companionship, career goals, everything else was left at the feet of Jesus. Chris, on the other hand, was very driven to make it in Hollywood. He immediately hired an agent and enrolled in acting classes. Because he was on the fast track to fame and I wasn't Chris thought I was lazy and unmotivated. He felt I should have been banging on doors to get back into radio but I just wasn't ready for any of that. Honestly, I wasn't sure I'd ever go back to deejaying again. I only knew one thing, I needed time with God. So each day I would spend long periods of time seeking His presence and basking in His love. My bedroom became my altar and there I lifted offerings of prayer, worship and adoration. Pursuing the Lord became my greatest passion, the deepest longing of my heart. I obsessed myself with Him and quit worrying about future plans. I didn't know exactly what was in the cards for me, only Who was dealing and that the deck was now stacked in my favor. And until I heard from the good Lord Himself, I'd be content to play Rook with the old folks.

Chapter 36

THE CHICK DOWNSTAIRS

At seventeen she was much too young to be out on her own. But she really didn't have much choice in the matter. Her parents had separated, vacated and were pursuing divorce. The family home went up for sale. Mom left California for Philly to stay with relatives. Dad rented a small apartment in downtown L.A., near the jail where he served as the staff psychiatrist. Their daughter somehow got lost in the shuffle. The best her folks could do under these sorrowful circumstances was help their daughter rent a place of her own. So Christy, just a few months shy of 'legal' adulthood, moved into the apartment complex on Topanga Canyon Boulevard, into the unit directly below mine. It was just her... her and a cat named Buffle. I had Christy pegged the first time I saw her. I even told her so. "You look like the type that burns incense and listens to Joni Mitchell," I teased. I wasn't into either but I could easily tell she was. It turned out that I was right on both counts. Some might call it a lucky guess but I say she looked the part with her long brunette hair, gauze wrap around skirts and spaghetti strap tank tops. Christy was the proverbial hippy chick, definitely my type, but just a wee bit too young.

"Keep moving 'em in, Wally!" I shouted to the apartment manager as he escorted Christy to the empty bachelor pad she'd soon call home. "Terry's the resident Romeo around here," he jested with a hearty laugh. The next time she saw me I was with a girlfriend. The next time she saw me I was with different girlfriend. After that she saw me on the balcony talking to the girl next door. Somehow she got the impression I was a ladies man. It is understandable why she would come to this crazy conclusion but I had no choice but to plead innocent to these scandalous charges. My only defense was, "It's not what you think." But most girls have heard that one before, even at the young age of seventeen. In spite of how things may have looked initially, Christy soon came to realize that I wasn't a player. Not the kind she thought anyway. I was only a harmless card player who engaged in a game called Rook with old folks.

When Christy invited me to her eighteenth birthday party at her apartment I told her I'd try to make it. "I don't get home until about 2:00AM," I explained. "It will still be going," she assured me with a hopeful smile. It was. She made everybody stay until I arrived. Oddly enough, they all left as soon as I got there... exactly as she had planned. And there I was, left alone with this young and pretty hippy chick close to me in the narrow hallway of her now quiet bachelor pad. We talked for hours... Hours upon hours all the way into the wee hours we talked and talked and talked. Up until this point we had never really conversed before, just casual chit-chat. But now we were getting deep, exchanging interests, ideas and dreams. Essentially, we were getting to know each other. It was like she could see into my heart and I could see into hers. I did not intend to fall in love that night but I did. We did. It was bound to happen. We had everything in common: music, art, the beach. Unknowingly, we even hung out at the very same beach, where all the hippy types clustered, a small stretch of sand where Topanga Canyon empties onto the coast. I took her there the very next day. And I saw her the day after that and the day after that. Every day, every spare moment of the day, we were together.

Though I felt I could talk about most anything with Christy, there was one thing I had neglected to share with her - my faith. It's not that I was hiding it, mind you. It's just that the subject never really came up. Maybe it should have before discussing interests like favorite foods, favorite songs and favorite artists but it didn't. Besides, we had only been seeing each other for about a week or so. These things take time, especially for a reserved fellow like me. There was much to deliberate, I had to think things through like; what to say, what not to say and when to say what I say. Okay, okay, maybe I was a bit of a closet Christian. But she eventually got the Truth out of me.

"Where are you going?" Christy inquired as I passed her by at the pool area.
"To uh... a meeting," I bashfully replied.
"What kind of meeting?" she pressed.
The word "Church." slowly rolled off my tongue while I nervously watched for any sudden signs of indifference.
To my surprise a smile swept over her face. "Can I go?" she pleaded.

They were three little words, comprised of a total of six measly letters, each dangling helplessly from a question mark twice their size. Yet the tiny plea had my heart doing cartwheels of colossal proportions. It was something I just didn't expect but, wow, was I ever elated when she popped the question. It was an appeal which would prove to change destiny for both of us. Without any reservation I complied with her request and took Christy with me to the Wednesday night service at Rancho por Dios.

Hand-in-hand we made our way into the small fellowship which I had grown to love so dearly. It didn't take long at all for Christy to fit right in. Everyone went to great measures to make her feel welcome as they did with me when I first visited. It's that 'love thing' I mentioned earlier. It's really quite infectious and this time the carriers were spreading it fast and furiously toward my girl. I think she could really identify with these folks too. They weren't any different than the sun soakers who hung out at Topanga Beach. They just happened to wear more clothing. But

199

the shine on their faces was plain to see. They radiated with joy under the warmth of God's precious Son. Christy, too, was being drawn to the light. She tasted of this divine love and longed for more. After the Bible study a gal named Bonnie shared the gospel with her. "Would you like to receive Jesus?" she asked Christy. "I want what Terry has," she beamed. Before long Bonnie was leading Christy into a prayer to receive Jesus Christ as her personal Lord and Savior.

Now that Christy was a fellow believer and sister in the Lord we had even more in common. I should clarify that; in Jesus we had everything in common. Because of Him our souls were knit closer and closer and our hearts were dancing to the same happy rhythm. So much so we became inseparable. Together we went to Rancho por Dios every Sunday morning and Wednesday evening. Besides fellowshipping at church we followed each other here, there and everywhere. We were like two magnets, one in tow of the other. With her living downstairs it just made it all the more convenient. We ate our meals together, hung out by the pool, watched TV and listened to music and prayed together - the whole shebang. We did absolutely everything as a couple. And with each passing day our hearts grew more and more in love. Christy became my dearest friend. I never knew what it was like to be so cared for until I met her. She complemented my life like a warm blanket to a shivering soul. We were so compatible and found our greatest joy in each other's company.

Following Christy's conversion everything happened rather quickly. Within a couple of months we were already talking about little yellow houses with white picket fences. There really wasn't any debate as to whether we should or shouldn't marry. We both understood this as our destiny. There just wasn't any way around it, we were meant to be joined as one for always.

Neither of us could imagine spending our lives apart. Fate would have us growing old together and teaming up in endless games of Rook by some sunny poolside. Our love was unquenchable, our longing was undeniable. So, on June 7, 1980, no less than eleven months after we fell in love on her birthday, we were united as one in an outdoor wedding in Calabasas, California.

With Christy at my side and the Lord in our hearts I felt the time was right to refocus on a career in radio. I only sent out one demo tape, to a country western station in the Palm Springs area. Shortly thereafter I was interviewed then hired. We had not even been married two months before Christy and I were bidding farewell to all our dear friends at Rancho por Dios. It was on her birthday, July 27, 1980, exactly one year after we fell in love, we moved from the apartment complex on Topanga Canyon to our new home in the sunny desert. To this day we still live happily ever after. And so we shall... till death do us part.

A FINAL THOUGHT

"We must put on faith and love as a breastplate and the hope of salvation as a helmet."
1 Thessalonians 5:8b

Both experience and scripture have taught me that for any relationship to flourish between two people the conditions must be right. For example, the ideal conditions for a successful marriage are faith, hope and love. You will discover that these are the 'big three' of the Bible as well. Let's deal with faith first. Faith simply says, "I believe in you and always will." Obviously, a bride and groom are headed for disaster if they can't make that declaration to one another. A marriage that is not built on trust is not a marriage at all. Faith is also a condition for a relationship with the Lord. (See John 3:16 and Ephesians 2:8)

A couple must also have the hope that they will remain together for always (in sickness and in health, in poverty and in wealth, for better or for worse.) There is a close tie between faith and hope. This is well noted in Hebrews eleven verse one where it states that "Faith is the substance of things hoped for." Hope is not the same as wishful thinking. When someone says, "I hope I win the lottery!" he readily accepts the fact that he may not. It's nothing more than a wish. But this is not the kind of hope the Bible talks about, nor is it the kind of hope a marriage is founded upon. The word used for hope in the New Testament is 'elpis'. It is the Greek term for 'expectation'. Couples enter into marriage with the expectation of growing old together. It's 'till death do you part.'

To say that love is a condition for marriage sounds like I'm stating the obvious. But I would remind the reader that the

Bible's definition of love is not anything like the world's definition of it. The world's view of love is upside-down. It says, "Me first, then others, then (maybe) God." Biblical love says the exact opposite, "God first, then others and me last." This is the divine order of agape love and it is a love that is unconditional. In other words, it loves according to this divine principle no matter what. This is why wedding rings are exchanged between bride and groom. Just like a circle has no end, neither should the love between husband and wife.

Faith, hope and love form the basis of the marriage covenant. They are echoed in the vows and they are the conditions for a relationship to flourish. It is for this reason that some couples would rather live together than 'tie the knot.' They lack the confidence in their partner or in themselves to exchange vows because they lack faith, or hope, or love. And even if you lack just one of these conditions 'till death do you part' becomes a frightening proposition.

I speak in terms of marriage because that is exactly the kind of relationship we enter into with Christ. When we accept Jesus as Lord and Savior we become to Him His bride. The conditions for this relationship to flourish are exactly the same as the ones we've already been discussing. We walk by faith trusting Jesus every step of the way. We have the wonderful hope of eternal life; it is not something we wish for but fully expect. And we love Him because He first loved us. Granted, our faith, hope and love is far from perfect when we enter into a relationship with the Lord. But that is what we strive for and Jesus helps us along the way. Honestly, without His help we would have no hope at all! Perhaps you are one who hesitates in making this kind of commitment to Christ. Maybe it's because you lack confidence in yourself. I would submit to you that that lack of self confidence is a good thing. The faith, hope and love I speak of is beyond man's reach. We have no other recourse but to look to Jesus. Let Him help you.

"So these three things remain: faith, hope, and love. But the best one of these is love." - 1 Corinthians 13:13

* * * * *

There is another reoccurring theme in my story and I hope it has pulled on a heartstring or two. The theme which I refer to is that of 'forgiveness'. Forgiveness is one of those things which love does. Love keeps no record of wrong (See 1 Corinthians 13:5). For forgiveness to come full circle we must receive it, accept it then give it. To receive forgiveness we must confess our sins to the Lord. As we accept His forgiveness we learn to forgive ourselves. Finally, we must forgive those who have sinned against us. You may want to think of forgiveness as a release valve. All the hurts, heartbreaks and abuses we suffer in life have a way of fueling up a lot of negative energy like hatred, anger and bitterness. If this negative energy is not released our souls stew until they boil and we are left miserable on the inside. There is only one release valve – forgiveness. "But I just don't have the capacity to forgive," you say. You're right, no one does. Forgiveness requires a supernatural ability. Our flesh would rather stew and it does everything to resist the act of forgiveness. That is exactly why we need Jesus.

Not too many years ago I was betrayed by someone very dear to me. I was terribly hurt and forgiveness was not my immediate response. As a matter of a fact, I just couldn't find it in me to forgive. What I did was pray. I was honest with God and told him I was too hurt to pardon the one who had betrayed me. However, knowing that unforgiveness does not please God, and realizing that it is a manifestation of utter hypocrisy in the Christian life, I pleaded with the Lord that He would grant me the power to forgive. Praying this prayer gave me a compassion for my betrayer. I began to pity him. Soon, I was praying for blessing upon His life. I have since seen the effects of this prayer both in his life and in mine. Furthermore, he has repented and we have been reconciled. I share this to assure you - the one who benefits most from forgiveness is you. The one who suffers most if you don't forgive is also you. While forgiveness does not come naturally to any of us, we do have help from above. Ask God to help you.

*   *   *   *   *

For my story to be told it was necessary to dig up a lot of dirt. I have shared of abuses, hurts and betrayals. But, far be it from this clod to throw stones at anyone. My sin stinks just as bad as the next person's. There is only one hero in my story and that is God. It is only by His grace that I've been saved from the mire. By His grace there is forgiveness for the molester, the abuser, the pornographer and the accuser. There is grace and forgiveness for all.

My story is true. Names have been changed to protect those I've forgiven.

*   *   *   *   *

"God is faithful and reliable. If we confess our sins, he forgives them and cleanses us from everything we've done wrong."
1 John 1:9

ACKNOWLEDGEMENTS

Very special thanks to:
My editor and dear friend Eric Gross. The pictures in this photo album were initially very rough. (See preface) His hours on the framework brought life and beauty to them.
My mom for all her sacrificial love.
Stan Angel for proclaiming good news.
Jim Allison, Rev. Harrah and Ric Wonders for the seeds planted.
Jimmy Van Patten for being my friend when no one else would be, and all the Van Patten's for showing me the value of family.
Gordo for the mercy and the lamb.
Jeff Kaplan for persevering and leading me into a right relationship with Jesus Christ.
Chris Feltman for the shower use up north and rooming with me down south.
Christy Michaels for her love and faithfulness.
Carly and Birdie for the joy they bring me.

ABOUT THE AUTHOR

Terry Michaels has had the privilege of serving in ministry for many years. He worked extensively with youth at *Calvary Chapel San Bernardino* in California and *Calvary Chapel Siegen* in Germany. Terry also served as founding pastor of *Calvary Chapel of the Springs* in San Marcos, Texas and currently pastors at *Calvary Austin*. Terry also has a background in broadcasting. He worked as a radio personality in California area markets such as Palm Springs, San Bernardino/Riverside and Mendocino. He is author of four books. Terry resides with his wife, Christy, in Austin. They have two daughters and a granddaughter.
www.terrymichaels.org
www.calvaryaustin.com

10132477R00127

Made in the USA
Charleston, SC
09 November 2011